Jan de luz

The FRENCH TOUCH

Unless mistreated, carved stone ages only toward beauty. The large sculpted vase is eighteenth century, in limestone from Bordeaux, as is the spherical pinnacle (top ornament for a pillar). The lustre (chandelier) and the sconce (barely visible) are both Napoleon III. Atop a wooden balcony railing salvaged from a hôtel particulier in Avignon, a bronze cheval is high-tailing it. The male figure is a store mannequin from the early art deco period.

The FRENCH TOUCH

Jan de Luz

Gibbs Smith, Publisher
Salt Lake City

First Edition
08 07 06 05 04   10 9 8 7 6 5 4 3 2 1

Text © 2004 Jan de Luz
Photographs © 2004 Tom O'Neal, unless otherwise noted

Published by
Gibbs Smith, Publisher
P.O. Box 667
Layton, Utah 84041

www.gibbs-smith.com
Orders: 1.800.748.5439

Jacket designed by Traci O'Very Covey
Interior designed by Traci O'Very Covey and Dawn DeVries Sokol

Printed and bound in Hong Kong

Library of Congress Control Number: 2004107214

ISBN 1-58685-367-8

FRONT JACKET: *This Renaissance beauty (circa 1600) weighs more than a ton and stands 7 x 6.5 x 3.4 feet (2,13 m wide x 2 m high x 1,4 m deep), in limestone quarried near Poitiers. She came from the Orléans region, south of Paris, and is now an impact feature of Jon Hagstrom's Villa La Duce in Carmel, California. The* frise à enroulement *(scrolling border) and* médaillon à profils *(cameo) on the* linteau *(mantel) and the* galbé *(deep curve) on the* jambage *(leg) are traditional features of Renaissance* cheminées *(fireplaces). The firebox was built by mason Ray Marzorini.* BACK JACKET: *Les pigeonniers (pigeon houses or pigeon towers) are found on farmlands throughout France, especially in the Midi Pyrénées. Almost all are separate structures; many are elaborate. In earliest times, royalty alone were allowed to maintain* pigeonniers. *Later, as provincial pride turned on having a healthy, fecund supply of pigeons for trading and as the rural messenger system, any farmers could own one. Access to the family* pigeonnier *became an important part of a daughter's dowry. In addition to their service as messengers until after World War I, pigeons were coddled because young pigeon meat is delicious and nutritious, and pigeon manure is prized by* les vignerons *(grape farmers) as an excellent fertilizer for grapes. This pigeonnier, built in the square-tower style, serves as the children's playhouse at the home of Jim and Mary Beth Crowley in Rancho Santa Fe, California.*

A MON AMI, Michel Bordagaray, et tous mes vrais amis basques dont l'état d'esprit et la culture ont été et seront toujours une source d'inspiration.

*This photograph proves the oft-told advice:
during an earthquake, stand in a doorway.
The roof of this neglected* maison de maître
*fell in. There was little of salvage value
beyond this wonderful (and strong) limestone door surround. It is now in Scottsdale,
Arizona, where it will become part of the
entry to a new home designed by Bing Hu
for John and Mary Cooper. The* chapiteau
(top ornament) marks it as a Régence.

CONTENTS

ACKNOWLEDGMENTS

IT'S A FOOL'S AMNESIA to forget to show appreciation to those who help you, and no one accomplishes much without the vital assistance of others. Even the lonely artist in his garret can validly thank nature herself for imagination. Arrogance or selfishness only blinds people to how much we need one another.

Since this book touches on endeavors throughout my adult life, there are far too many people to acknowledge individually. These include Basque farmers, some now dead; artisans willing to share secrets of craft; every customer, because reputation is built in part by the loyalty of others; the staff and supporters who helped bring the *éco-musée* to life; and the early weavers who worked long hours, sometimes in dim light but with beaming smiles and a shared belief in what I was trying to accomplish. I hold thousands of people in a grateful heart.

Some people deserve specific mention, though, because their help was essential to the completion of this book. These include the architects, designers and homeowners who participated—especially Michael Layne, for a spirited Foreword and his tremendous goodwill; Michael Bolton; Paul Davis; John Matthams; Charles Gruwell; Dana Beach; Greg and Kate Blackwell; Lee Caplin and Gita Karasik; John and Mary Cooper; Jim and Mary Beth Crowley; Jack and Gayle Daniels; Bruce and Karyn DeBoer; Jacques Denarnaud; Frank and Marilyn Dorsa; Jon Hagstrom; Lee and Becky Hofmann; Bob and Glynne Lewis; John and Maureen Machado; Norman and Nancy Nason; George Veazey and Stephanie Mower; Eduardo Venegas and Karen Weinberg-Venegas; Richard and Hildegard Wax; Michael and Kira Whitaker; and, the clock master Switzerland must cry to have lost, Walter Loeliger. Neither this book nor my business would exist without the friendship and trust of people in the industry.

Without Tom O'Neal's talent with a camera, this book would be but flat tales. Thank you, Tom, for the beautiful photographs and for your enthusiasm throughout the project.

I would be remiss not to acknowledge the masters of talent at Gibbs Smith, Publisher: my editor, Madge Baird; designers Traci O'Very Covey and Dawn Sokol; Alison Einerson, Molly Douma and their marketing team; Christopher Robbins; and the fine Gibbs Smith himself.

Sandrine Lardit is simply aces as a French-English translator, and leads with a generous and cheerful demeanor. Mark Kane kept the computers, scanners and printers behaving, which is both vital and not easy, unless you speak their language. Thankfully, he does, always with humor and patience. Michele sets an example for smooth precision in managing the St. Helena store. *Michele, nous t'aimons.* Char Etienne has contributed more to the development of the Carmel Valley store than surely I acknowledge, especially as the days get busier and I bark faster. And truly, to every employee, whose knowledge and energy are the very qualities that build the stores, I say thank you again and again. Without quality employees, we cannot build clientele.

Roy Woods is singularly responsible for our fantastic location in Carmel Valley. His kindness surely makes the angels smile. And Jacques, the depth of my gratitude for your loyalty and constancy is immeasurable.

Finally, from inside my heart arise love and appreciation for my children, Carla, Léhéna and Olivier, and my beloved wife, Brigitte, who not only takes care of me heart and soul but also manages the retail stores and so many day-to-day details that I have time for creative projects such as this book. For me, family is the bright morning of each day and the enveloping satisfaction of all effort. *Famille, je vous aime.*

PHOTOGRAPHER'S NOTES

I HAVE BEEN PHOTOGRAPHING ARCHITECTURAL details for years, yet working on this book with Jan has opened another depth of perception. Now I see that inanimate objects can have character and become alive, if seen with knowing eyes. Each piece has its own story to tell.

Looking at a fireplace from the time of Louis XIII in a modern surrounding is an extraordinary experience. It is like walking through a portal of time—the presence of history, of lives and their stories lost in the mists of time; how fragile people are compared to the substance and strength of stone. These sensations open awareness to creating your own story, for these times.

Also fascinating is the craftsmanship. The items have workmanship that reveals a different dedication than typical today. It has humbled me to see how people could create such beautiful carvings, stonework, sculpture and details all by hand. The value of each artist's work has carried through centuries.

—TOM O'NEAL
CARMEL VALLEY, CALIFORNIA
www.tgophoto.com

FOREWORD

Jan de Luz travels France to ferret out the unusual and useful. His passion for the wonders of the French past surrounds him with found items of stately elegance and simple country craftsmanship. These resurrected and restored treasures touch our memories and bring back warm and precious encounters with rural France.

Years ago on a trip through Provence, a dusty village clinging to a scrubby hillside olive orchard beckoned. It was hot and I was thirsty. I parked at the edge of the village square under the canopy of an ancient London plane tree. The shade brought relief, and I paused to study the worn textural patina of the shops circling the square. Before me was a visual buffet and my architectural mind digested each vignette with ravishing pleasure. A *boulangerie* tempted with a window full of lovingly displayed breads and pastries. I studied the façade; there was a faded gold-leaf sign above the poured glass windows. The windows had puttied glazing and the wood was coated layer upon layer with a peeling glossy black paint. Below the windows, a pair of stain-oxidized pewter planters flanking a wood-and-iron bench overflowed with red geraniums. The Dutch door, matching the windows, was a crinkled black and half open. The smell of fermenting yeast and warm brioche threatened to draw me out from the shade.

Across the square, the laughter of children saved me from the temptation of the bakery. Children were playing at the village fountain. They looked properly French in their striped T-shirts, dark shorts, sandals and handkerchief caps knotted at each corner. They were drawn to the fountain's cool, clear water. I knew that years ago women would have gathered to fill buckets or wash clothes and share daily gossip. Plumbing has changed that tradition, but the children still needed the fountain as they confronted the heat of the afternoon sun by splashing water on each other.

As the game of splashing continued, I marveled at the patina and textures that aging had painted across the fountain's stone surface.

What had the fountain witnessed?

There were clues. The water poured from four spigots that jutted out like rusted goosenecks from a carved and beveled limestone column. The stone column positioned itself like a monolith in the center of the fountain's octagonal basin. The column was capped with a chipped stone pedestal supporting a limestone sphere. The basin was at least ten feet across and high enough and wide enough to sit on. I noticed the spigots didn't exactly match and one looked much newer than the rest. Had one been stolen or just broken beyond repair?

The basin, too, had been patched. Were the chips and missing chunks from collisions with old carts or the clumsy machinery of war? The war had come through the village. Pockmarks from shrapnel and gunfire punctuated the complexion of the stone, memorializing the events of history and lending it character.

I had all but forgotten that day in that small French village until clients discovered an old limestone fountain at the Carmel Valley store of Jan de Luz. The sight of it brought them instant joy and they decided yes. Jan had it boxed and trucked to their home in Los Gatos. There it was unpacked and assembled in its new position as the central element in their circular drive and the cobblestone entry to their Provence-inspired house.

The octagonal basin was waterproofed and then filled with water; around it a flower bed was planted with lavender. We flipped a switch and water began to flow out of the rusty gooseneck spigots. The moment was magic. This old resurrected fountain that once served a village and its people was now central in the life of another family. It may even have been the same fountain from that little village. The pockmarks were there, as were the chips and patches.

Whatever the history of this fountain, its presence evokes warmth and respect. It tells its story to a newer generation and lives on as link to the past. This, I feel, is the understated value of Jan de Luz's found relics, whether they are grand fountains and massive fireplaces or subtle, like old, worn chestnut flooring, or practical, like a marble-topped pastry table. Their vitality arises from the substance of the stories they hold.

The French sensibility includes a subtle, harmonious marriage of quaint antiquity and the demanding present—the combining of distant generations, the new and the old, hand in hand, contemplation of the future and reminiscence of the past, a child sitting on a great-grandparent's lap listening to an old family tale.

Jan de Luz brings to life these images and ignites an appreciation for the quality and craftsmanship of an earlier time. He provides the design world a broad spectrum of precious elements, which allows us to craft warm and welcoming homes. These elements give substance and validation to our designs, and the visions they fire touch the soul.

—MICHAEL LAYNE
ST. HELENA, CALIFORNIA

STYLE AS POINT OF VIEW

THE CRITIC KENNETH TYNAN DESCRIBED LITERARY STYLE AS "THE EFFORTLESS PRESENTATION OF CONTENT." HE WAS SPEAKING OF WRITING, BUT THIS IS JUST AS TRUE FOR ALL FORMS OF ART, INCLUDING A PERSON'S LIFESTYLE, BUSINESS STYLE, PARENTING STYLE, AND ALL PERSONAL CHOICES. LIFE IS THE CANVAS, AND STYLE IS THE GROOMING OF POINT OF VIEW. ⌁ One sunny day, a genial man ventured into the warehouse in Carmel Valley, California. While I was involved in finding space for new pieces in from France, I am never too busy to welcome a prospective customer, this time a homeowner getting away from the dust and noise of remodeling his home by taking a drive. As fate would have it (and fate

Customers are the "angels" of every business, and I am blessed. These stone angels are from the eighteenth century. Made to grace the entrance to a presbyter, they are a real pair (each figure individually sculpted and the two looking at each other).

297

RUE DES
PASTOUREAUX

Cell door from a 150-cell jail near Toulouse, France, constructed of pitchpin (yellow pine), with closable iron eyehole, sliding door for food service and working lock with key, in its original surround of Belgium bluestone. It is perfect now as a secure street entrance to the garden at the home of Eduardo Venegas and Karen Weinberg-Venegas in Carmel, California.

From a distance, the Belgian bluestone looks strong and, when the sun is low, nearly luminescent. Close up, it delights again with texture and craft.

does have her way), he found several things he liked, and I found a friend, Eduardo Venegas.

This is how life works: you go to work every day, preferably doing something you enjoy, and life pays you back. At least that's what I've discovered repeatedly.

Ed found a half dozen pieces he liked, and the directness with which he selected and installed them illustrates my belief that knowing what you like and being bold can serve utility and self-expression equally well. I haven't asked Ed if he agrees with me—that style is the lifelong grooming of point of view—but my guess is that he would smile an agreement.

His first choice—a jail cell door—was straightforward. He liked it right away and was eager to join its "rescue team." The only decision was whether it would best serve as an exterior door to the house or as the street entrance to the garden. He chose the garden, because the door's "guard dog hardware" seemed more natural as the most exterior access to the home, and because in the garden he could more easily incorporate its authentic surround of Belgium bluestone, itself a beautiful feature.

Ed's sense that he was joining a rescue team means a lot to me. In a very real way, each customer becomes an extension of my goal: to find fine architectural antiques before they are destroyed or eroded beyond the point of usefulness and relocate them to safe places where they can begin being beautiful and serviceable for another century or three.

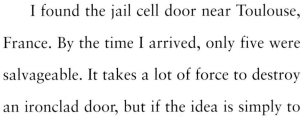

LEFT: *Detail of working lock, more than 200 years old, on jail cell door from near Toulouse, France. The jail had more than 150 cells, but by the time I arrived, builders in a hurry to "rip and build" had destroyed all but five, which I eagerly rescued.* RIGHT: *Detail of closable iron eyehole. Even in France 200 years ago, prisoners would spit at guards if they could; hence the glass piece, now aged beautifully green, with working retractable closure.* OPPOSITE: *The ironclad side of the cell door that once faced prisoners is now framed by ivy and evergreens. It is still strong and imposing, if less forlorn, and its age is only another asset, like the original Belgian bluestone surround.*

I found the jail cell door near Toulouse, France. By the time I arrived, only five were salvageable. It takes a lot of force to destroy an ironclad door, but if the idea is simply to tear down rather than dismantle, two hundred years of strength can be twisted into uselessness in about five seconds.

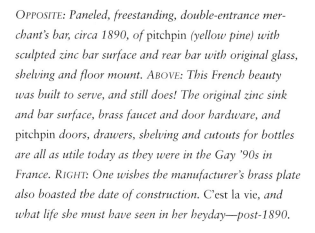

OPPOSITE: *Paneled, freestanding, double-entrance merchant's bar, circa 1890, of* pitchpin *(yellow pine) with sculpted zinc bar surface and rear bar with original glass, shelving and floor mount.* ABOVE: *This French beauty was built to serve, and still does! The original zinc sink and bar surface, brass faucet and door hardware, and* pitchpin *doors, drawers, shelving and cutouts for bottles are all as utile today as they were in the Gay '90s in France.* RIGHT: *One wishes the manufacturer's brass plate also boasted the date of construction.* C'est la vie, *and what life she must have seen in her heyday—post-1890.*

I don't mean to be overly dramatic. Not everything two hundred years old is worth saving, and some of today's designs are as worthy as the old pieces I hunt down. There *are* modern pieces that will serve utility with beauty for their own few hundred years of distinction, but creating new beauty does not absolve us from the civility of respect.

There's no doubt Ed understood the spirit and practicality of the task he assigned himself. One might offer that the door, originally intended as merely sternly useful, is now beautiful as well. Doors do not have pride, even if one is tempted to claim the door now "proudly" guards the Venegas garden, but I do feel Ed has a right to enjoy and take pride in how well he accomplished his rescue mission.

Old bars are a favorite for remodelers and new constructors alike, which guarantees they will stay scarce, and to find one that has all components—sink and faucets in working order, back bar with shelving still intact, mirror unbroken, with complete and sound mounting base—is truly rare. This was the second piece Ed Venegas spotted in the warehouse that day—a merchant's bar from Reims, France, east of Paris, circa 1890.

Twelve-foot circular staircase, circa 1850, retrieved from Lille, France, where it once served as the stairs from kitchen to bedroom in a small town house. Handmade of cured alder that wraps alder treads and matching lathed balustrade, it stands as a thing of beauty.

Actually, it wasn't hard to spot; it stands out. "Boy, she's something," he said right away. By the time he had finished eyeing, stroking and contemplating, he announced her "a beauty." She would "dress up" the living room, he said, with the mirror shined and glassware gleaming on the shelves. What could be more festive? Now, having lived with her for two years, Ed and his wife, Karen, declare the convenience is even better than her beauty. One doesn't need a party to enjoy the advantage of water, a sink and a serving surface for everyday snacks and lunches.

OLD BARS ARE A FAVORITE FOR REMODELERS AND NEW CONSTRUCTORS ALIKE, WHICH GUARANTEES THEY WILL STAY SCARCE, AND TO FIND ONE THAT HAS ALL COMPONENTS . . . IS TRULY RARE.

The *pièce de résistance*, though, was and always will be the third piece Ed chose: a twelve-foot circular staircase. He wasn't sure, at first. After all, their home doesn't have a second story, so where would it go? He didn't commit to this one right away, but the next day, having slept on it, he was ready. Ed knew then and has never wavered: A thing of beauty doesn't need to "go" anywhere, or to "do" anything; it only needs to "be" . . . in his home, as soon as possible.

There it stands now—stately, impressive, unspeakably lovely—as a piece of art in the living room, a grand wrap of whimsy that celebrates self-expression from any angle.

This kind of bold self-acceptance is integral to my view of style as a grooming of point of view. One doesn't need to have Ed Venegas's life experiences as a world traveler to have

an instinct for giving beauty its due, nor Karen Weinberg-Venegas's intelligence and humor to relish individualism. One only need look inside oneself, do what's necessary to like the view inside and then to love life. With those preconditions, the innate vigor of the life force and nature's own power of imagination will bring amazement and keep you productive. And if you learn how to stay in a state of amazement while being productive, you will be living, breathing style—your very own, inimitable style.

Maybe I'm too French, or too me, or just too much, but this is my view. This is the *French Touch* according to Jan de Luz.

LEFT: Side view of twelve-foot alder staircase, showing its steep rise and tight curl. ABOVE: Detail of the underside of the risers, still sound and strong after 150 years.

DESIGNING TRANSITIONS

A THRUM IS A FRINGE OF WARP THREADS LEFT ON THE LOOM AFTER REMOVING A WOVEN CLOTH. IT IS A SIGN, A VESTIGE OF EFFORT, LIKE SWEAT ON THE BROW OR DIRT UNDER THE FINGERNAILS. THIS IS THE STORY OF A MAN WHO SPOTTED A THRUM. THAT THRUM, TOGETHER WITH CURIOSITY AND THE WILLINGNESS TO WORK HARD, ALLOWED FATE TO WEAVE A WONDERFUL TALE. ✑ I was born in the Basque region of southwestern France. My first work, as an apprentice with expert cabinetmaker M. Lalanne, taught me pride in workmanship and

St. Jean de Luz, in the heart of the Basque region of Southwest France, possesses beauty and vitality in equal measures. Now a major tourist destination, its waterways carry as many personal watercraft as commercial these days. My first linen workshop grew up in a first-floor seaside room (right front corner of the building at the right in the photo) in the sixteenth-century House of the Infante, more famous actually as the temporary home of Marie-Thérèse d'Autriche "Infante d'Espagne" for a few months before she married King Louis XIV. The building is now home to the Musée Grévin, a branch of the famed Paris wax museum. (Photo by Jacques Denarnaud)

the honor of manual labor. Everyone—my parents and M. Lalanne, certainly—expected me to stick with this and become a cabinetmaker. Something in the heart refused. Instinct led elsewhere.

Playing hop-skip with history, I'll jump over the then-required stint in the French military and my successful lark of running one restaurant that led to the exhaustion of owning four, to a day in 1977 at the Bayonne auction. I was aware of an "itch"—a sense that I was looking for something new, but had no idea what. I went to the auction in Bayonne (the largest city in the French Basque region) for general enjoyment—to learn

something. Who knew what it would be? Not me, certainly. Although I am naturally goal-oriented, I also recognize that growth can come from spurts of vague desire, not always by design. Intuition is sometimes smarter than logic.

The rooster is ubiquitous in France as a symbol of earnest hope, a way of reminding ourselves to rise with the dawn and sing, for there is a new day of life for living. American writer Ralph Waldo Emerson was more didactic, but no less apt in expressing a spirit that builds both sanity and a productive life: Finish every day and be done with it. You have done what you could. Some blunders and absurdities, no doubt crept in. Forget them as soon as you can; tomorrow is a new day: begin it well and serenely with too high a spirit to be encumbered with your old nonsense.

The Bayonne auction is diverse. Part of the fun is digging around, looking for oddments. Set aside on the ground, I saw a pile of wood and metal with some bits of cloth on top, apparently an old Basque hand loom, for anyone wanting to try putting it together again. The wood looked good,

CHICKEN BASQUE STYLE

POULET BASQUAISE
Pour : 6 personnes
Préparation : 30 mn
Cuisson : 1 h 15
INGRÉDIENTS : 1 poulet (2 kg),
60 ml d'huile d'olive, 4 poivrons
pelés, 6 tomates pelées, 2 oignons,
3 échalotes, 1 bouquet garni,
2 gousses d'ail, 150 g jambon de
Bayonne, sel et poivre.

∽ Découpez le poulet en 12 morceaux.
∽ Faites-les dorer dans un sautoir et
dans l'huile, poivrez, salez.
∽ Ajoutez le jambon en morceaux et
les échalotes hachées. Quand c'est
doré, retirez du sautoir mais gardez
au chaud.
∽ Dans le jus de cuisson, faites revenir
les poivrons en lanières 8 à 10 mn,
puis ajoutez-les au poulet.
∽ Toujours dans le même jus, faites
blondir les oignons hachés, puis
ajoutez les tomates en dés, le bouquet et l'ail écrasé. Au bout de 10
mn, remettez le poulet, le jambon et
les poivrons. Couvrez et laissez
achever la cuisson.

CHICKEN BASQUE STYLE
For: 6 persons
Preparation time: 30 min
Cooking time: $1^1/4$ hour
INGREDIENTS: 1 chicken ($4^1/2$ lbs),
$^1/4$ cup olive oil, 4 peeled green
peppers, 6 peeled tomatoes,
2 onions, (chopped), 3 shallots,
1 bouquet garni (parsley, thyme,
fennel tied together), 2 garlic
cloves, 5 ounces Bayonne ham or
prosciutto, salt and pepper to taste

∽ Cut the chicken in 12 pieces.
∽ Fry in a pan with olive oil till golden;
add salt and pepper.
∽ Add the ham cut in pieces and the
minced shallots. When golden, take
out of the pan and keep warm.
∽ In the pan drippings, sauté the green
peppers cut in strips for 8-10 minutes, then add to chicken.
∽ In the same juices, let the chopped
onions cook till golden, then add the
tomatoes cut in cubes, the bouquet
and the crushed garlic. After 10 minutes, return the chicken with ham
and the green peppers. Cover and
finish cooking.

but there was no way to be sure all the parts were there. And why would I want an old Basque loom? I'd never woven anything, or had an idea I ever would; but it seemed full of life. Someone had used it, worked and produced useful things with it for years. For some reason, I raised my hand to bid. There was no competition. I bought it for hardly anything.

I carried the loom home to my garage and immediately started laying out the pieces.

ASSEMBLING THE LOOM WASN'T EASY. I HAD TO FEEL MY WAY, OFTEN REALIZING THE VALUE OF TECHNIQUE I'D LEARNED WITH M. LALANNE.

Eager to find out if I could figure it out, I was suddenly aware that while I had worn clothes all my life, bought restaurant linens, knew what type of bath towels I liked, and knew cloth was, well, part of the fabric of life, I had never seriously thought about how cloth was made. I don't know why, but that day a new fascination lit my heart.

Assembling the loom wasn't easy. I had to feel my way, often realizing the value of technique I'd learned with M. Lalanne. Figuring out what each piece did and how the whole worked together wasn't easy and required a huge amount of time—absorbing all the spare hours for nearly four months—but it was challenging and interesting.

As I worked, I thought about the process of weaving and decided I would try to re-create the piece of fabric that remained in *les lices*, a piece of flat-woven, natural linen with seven blue stripes of varying widths. I took the bit of cloth to a *bouvier* (cattleman) in Urrugne (Basque cattle country), who confirmed that it was, indeed, part of a *mante à bœuf*—a traditional Basque cattle blanket put on *after* the morning climb up the Pyrenees to the fields. The cattle would get hot walking

Once assembled, it required days to figure out how to prepare the "teeth" of the comb that creates the texture you intend. At the rate of six feet a day, if you work hard, the small inventory on the rear shelves represents some serious time, and not much time lost to repairing ropes that shift the shuttle. Foot pedals direct the shuttle motion. The weaving operation requires constant attention, especially for consistency, but it is not physical as much as time-bound. (Photo by Jan de Luz)

up the mountain. The *mantes à bœuf* absorbed the sweat, slowing the cooling and protected the animals from the hot sun. A caring *bouvier* would also tie on cloth or lamb's wool eye shields to protect from pestering flies, allowing the cattle to rest more favorably.

A few days later, I went to the museum in Bayonne to do more research. I learned that the seven stripes signified the seven Basque provinces; that each color identified a village; and that the width of the stripes indicated the wealth of the landowner.

In ancestral times, most Basque farms were virtually self-sufficient. Along with the usual assortment of farm animals, an orchard and vegetable garden, farmers planted flax. The Pyrenees have a good climate for flax because of their humidity. When textile weavers

needed great volumes of linen, they moved flax production to flatter country in northern France, Belgium and Ireland. For self-sufficient farmers in the Pyrenees, though, flax makes linen, and cloth was as essential for survival as the work animals. When harvested and dried, a member of the family or an itinerant weaver would clean, thread and weave the flax, supplying the cloth

Communal picnics are basic to Basque family life. Here, my family and I are in the country with a bouvier and his team, decked in mantes à bœuf and eye shields. Traditionally, at four o'clock each day, everyone pauses for a piece of bread, sheep's-milk cheese and cherry jam with family, neighbors or coworkers. (Photo by Jan de Luz)

LA PIPERADE

LA PIPERADE

Pour : 4 personnes
Préparation : 25 mn
Cuisson : 45 mn
INGRÉDIENTS : 10 piments verts,
huile d'olive, 2 gousses d'ail,
1 oignon, 1 piment fort, 4 tomates,
6 œufs, persil, 4 tranches de jambon
de Bayonne

⁂ Epépinez et coupez les piments.

⁂ Faites-les dorer à feu doux dans
l'huile d'olive tiède (pour leur éviter
de noircir) avec l'ail, l'oignon et le
piment fort.

⁂ Ajoutez les tomates après les avoir
plongées dans l'eau bouillante pour
les peler plus facilement et laissez
réduire le tout environ 1/2 heure.

⁂ Battez les œufs en omelette avec
une pincée de sel et le persil haché.
Ajoutez-les à la préparation
précédente. Laissez cuire à feu
doux en remuant pour bien
brouiller les œufs.

⁂ Faites poêler séparément les tranches de jambon.

⁂ Servez la piperade dans un plat
chaud, garni avec le jambon.

PIPERADE

For: 4 persons
Preparation time: 25 min.
Cooking time: 45 min.
INGREDIENTS: 10 small green peppers,
olive oil, 2 garlic cloves, 1 onion,
1 chili pepper, 4 tomatoes, 6 eggs,
parsley, 4 slices of Bayonne ham or
prosciutto

⁂ Take out the seeds from the green
peppers and cut them in chunks.

⁂ Let them turn golden in warm olive
oil (to keep them from turning
black), with the garlic, the onion,
and the chili pepper.

⁂ Add the tomatoes, which have been
tossed in boiling water to facilitate
the peeling, and let everything boil
down for 1/2 hour.

⁂ Beat the eggs into an omelet with a
pinch of salt and the chopped
parsley. Add to the tomato mix.
Cook over low heat while stirring so
the eggs get scrambled.

⁂ Cook the ham in another pan.

⁂ Serve the piperade on a preheated
plate, accompanied by the ham.

needed for summer clothes, bedding, kitchen uses and animal care, including the *mantes à bœuf*. The larger farms would schedule an itinerant weaver to come to live on the farm for a fortnight or more to do that year's weaving.

Stoked with fresh knowledge about flax and weaving, I finished assembling the loom. All pieces still worked and seemed reasonably robust, but teaching myself how to weave well enough to match the cloth found with the loom was not easy. It was a good six months before I produced cloth that satisfied me. Through trial and error, I made

some small pieces, designing in my head a line of contemporary linens based on the ancestral design. Instinct told me others would like fine-quality linens that echoed a forgotten art.

The instinct proved itself. I sold my first major piece, a blue-striped tablecloth. Then I made another, and sold that one, too. Soon, I moved the loom down to the historic House of the Infante and set up shop, sitting by a window onto the port—weaving, designing, holding faith—and found that people not only stopped to watch, but came in to buy and to order particular items in specific dimensions. I hung finished pieces from the ceiling of the workshop, to wave in the breeze like a dream alive.

Flax production in the Basque country ended in the early 1900s, so I had to find sources from northern France, then also from Belgium and Ireland, and later from Romania, Poland, Russia and even China, always searching for the best available. I expanded the designs—from tablecloths, place mats and napkins, to aprons, dish towels and

Monogrammed napkins are very nice for entertaining. These napkins, custom embroidered at Jan de Luz, are done in the linen developed to re-create the texture of the mantes à bœuf. *The luxuriant texture surprises people. They can't resist crumpling the fabric, enjoying its texture and amazing "hand-feel."*

later bath towels, robes and blankets. With each new design came more customers and more ideas. I learned the art of producing the finest quality, and sales grew steadily. I opened a retail store in St. Jean de Luz, had to hire a production team, and was soon opening a second store about 35 miles (55 *kilomètres*) away in St. Jean Pied de Port, the starting point for *le chemin de Saint Jacques de Compostelle*, the famous pilgrimage through the Pyrenees for the devoted, history-minded and athletic.

As success grew, so did my gratitude for the provident instinct that had led me. Two stores became four. Designers were using my fabric for couture! Four shops popped to ten.

To stock the stores, I had to keep designing and managing steady production, of course, but also found a new joy—locating great old *vitrines* (store displays, usually glass-fronted), tables, chandeliers, benches and other furniture for the stores. This sent me gleefully into the country, to auctions and to estate sales, on the hunt for quality antiques.

OPPOSITE: *Dish towels hang from the ceiling in all Jan de Luz stores. I still like the way it looks, but it is also a lovely memory for me.* ABOVE: *In Basque country, the whole family helps. Here, my daughter, Carla, is adding grace and a smile to the launch of the bed collection. We needed to establish steady production of great quantities of linen to add the expanse of sheets to the line, and had to keep the blankets on the hand loom because they were too heavy for the mechanical looms. (Photo by Jacques Denarnaud)* OVERLEAF: *Dish towels embroidered in an array of Jan de Luz original designs, ready to last a lifetime of daily use.*

Often, I would return from these hunts to find that a customer wanted to buy one or more of the store displays. This was always happy news, for it gave me another trip into the country, and these explorations were always full of discovery. One of life's natural graces is that one good instinct leads to another.

Meanwhile, I kept thinking, especially when traveling through the countryside, how sad that so much Basque tradition was being lost in the pace and transitions of life. "How can we capture it?" I kept asking, until it became simply apparent. The way to do it is just to do it. A farm on *route nationale 10* on the way into St. Jean de Luz became available, and step by step—one problem solved, then over the next hurdle, with the help of friends and community—the first *éco-musée* in France opened, welcoming everyone to the traditional Basque culture and crafts.

I started with what I knew best—the ancestral needs of flax-to-linen production and *mantes à bœuf*. Then we added displays for the major elements of Basque culture—language, music, dance, architec-

ABOVE: Aprons are utile, unimpressive except in the purpose they serve. I added a style of apron within a year of moving the hand loom to the first workshop in the House of the Infante. When a third customer requested a different size, I started experimenting with how to make one style adjustable for all. After many failures, I had a design that was sturdy, functional and adaptable from children to the tallest man. We couldn't keep them in stock, and it wasn't long before my delightful solution had been copied by a dozen others. (Photo by Jan de Luz)
RIGHT: Jean-Charles de Castelbajac stopped by the éco-musée and asked a thousand questions. His enthusiasm reinvigorated even me. It was amazing! He kept in touch, and two seasons later he returned to select some designs for his haute couture collection. (Photo by Jan de Luz)

ture, food, sports—and detailed the original Basque crafts—the *espadrille* and *makila* (traditional walking stick made of medlar wood). And, because this is a Basque place, we created space for children to play. I was a happy, gratified man.

Let's hop over the pond now to America, and then across the wide country to California. I first saw Carmel Valley in 1979, coming over with my first sale of linens for an American restaurant, Casanova in Carmel, a fine restaurant owned by a

fine Belgian man, Walter Georis. I was bewitched. Deep in the Valley, the landscape has the premier virtue of looking a lot like the Pyrenees—mountains rolling down to the sea. These hills are not as high and tortuous as the Pyrenees, but evocative, and sunnier, warmer.

The dream of living here didn't evaporate. Almost two decades later, after being sure that my wife would love it, too, I sold the French stores and European production, and moved the family over in 1996.

ABOVE: *This table is set for a celebration, dressed in* Leiho Blanc. *The three-dimensional quality of the pattern is created by two factors: selection of the patterning thread and controlling the comb for maximum tightness on the stripes. The traditional* soupière en faïence *(porcelain tureen) is nineteenth century.*

In the eight years since unpacking the crates, we have established production of the linens, opened three company-owned retail stores and two licensees, and greatly expanded the second aspect of the business—antique furnishings and architectural elements.

Most exciting is the embracing American spirit. The liberty here is startling. The openness is demanding and refreshing. I delight in the irony that my business success relies on "young" America appreciating the quality of artisanal linens and antiques with the luxuriant patina of time.

OPPOSITE: Place mats (this design, "Jan de Luz Noir") are ideal for the informal breakfast or brunch. As the retail stores became established, we added housewares, such as glasses, dishes, salt and pepper mills and présentoirs. This bronze lady from a Marseille café appeared laden with freshly baked croissants or pastries for a century of mornings. LEFT: As a pre-teen, while friends were playing soccer or pelote basque, I was already prowling the flea markets, buying here and selling there, trying to turn a profit the same day. My family didn't have the money to give my brother and me "allowances," so I created ways to make my own money. This one is in Paris, but every French village has a street that becomes a market at least one day a week, if not every day. I lost the time to do this when the textile business started to roll; and so when the stores needed displays, I was thrilled to be out in the country, on the hunt again. When the building of the éco-musée began, I had to find truly representative pieces, tightening the standards. The challenge of quality is the best thing about learning: the more you learn, the more you know what you appreciate. And when you make a mistake, you learn faster because it means you lose money.

Hunting the Fine, the Rare, the Serviceable

Our days are a mixture of the grand and the gritty, the sublime and the ridiculous, the wondrous and the worrisome. Any thoughtful person beyond the age of puberty can think of a hundred opposites that merge into the composite we call life. The view any one person has is but through a peephole, a tiny view onto a vastness. Expanding the width of that peephole is the constant challenge, and an enduring joy.

Spring chairs became popular with the bourgeoisie in the early 1900s, when people finally had sufficient income and ease to have time to sit outdoors. We forget that for many centuries the prospect of anyone sitting idle outdoors was so unlikely that no one had conceived of furniture for such a rare event. This spring chair of good size was broken and faded, but still handsome even so.

RIGHT ABOVE: At 8 x 12 x 4 feet (2,4 m wide x 3,6 m x 1,2 m deep), this 1840 fireplace is large but not massive. Gothique to early-Renaissance fireplaces were often twice as large because they were used for cooking as much as for warmth. The godrons *on the* base de la tablette *and the* feuilles d'acanthe *on the* jambage *(leg) signify Renaissance influences. Savonnière limestone, with its remarkably fine-grained and stable texture, was favored for high-detail carving. Many pieces of bas-relief and haut-relief are in Savonnière. Only small amounts of raw Savonnière are still available; the quarries are mostly mined-out. It is now rare and expensive.*

RIGHT BELOW: The trumeau *(portion above the mantel, a part of the flue) carries the* sceau *(official seal of the family name). A well-flourished* fleur de lis *balances the* linteau *(mantel). Although large, this fireplace is well proportioned and so finely detailed she feels delicate. She will serve warmly again in a living, dining or great room.*

OVERLEAF: This bibliothèque de cloître *is an amazing 20 x 8 feet (6 m wide x 2,4 m high). Actually* pitchpin *(yellow pine), the wonderful walnut hue results from the effect of 150 years of regular waxing. The companion table in front is covered with protective paper. Unfortunately, the twenty-four chairs in the set no longer match. Here, in the warehouse of an estate buyer I deal with often, the cupboard sits next to a Canadian canoe almost as old. The horse-drawn* jardinière *in the foreground has springs, marking it as early 1900s. In fairly good shape, it was probably used by a* maraîcher *(vegetable farmer) to bring his produce to the village market.*

"Vision is the art of seeing what is invisible to others," in the words of Jonathan Swift. I wish he were still around and that I knew him. We could share some wine and cheese and a thousand stories. I would invite him to go along on my next buying trip, for that is when seeing all that is there is so very important—not just what is apparent, but all that there is.

THE TRUTH IS THAT ALL THE EASY FINDS HAVE BEEN FOUND. GREAT DISCOVERIES AWAIT, OF COURSE, BUT THEY WILL BE UNCOVERED BY EXPERTS WILLING TO WORK HARDER THAN IN THE PAST.

On the good side, there is beauty buried under swipes of paint or long forgotten in cobwebby attics. Dangers abound as well—hidden damage caused by subsidence, water or other erosions that even the best restoration artist cannot fix. The skill of discovery and the quality of discernment are the two most important aspects of this business.

The truth is that all the easy finds have been found. Great discoveries await, of course, but they will be uncovered by experts willing to work harder than in the past. More time, more travel, more research, more scouring. These experts also must be able to see beyond the mistakes people have made and how to correct those mistakes, some of which are truly horrendous but still fixable. This is the real *salvaging* part of my business and I love that.

It can be a huge amount of work. Depending on the nature of the problem—layers of paint that should never have been there, a horrid amount of encrusted soot, a missing nose or lion's paw, holes poked through to accommodate haphazard modernization—correcting the mistakes sometimes requires a team of six or eight restoration experts, each a specialist in some aspect of cleaning and mending.

A typical example is the wonderful Renaissance fireplace I found in Marne. The building, abandoned decades before, was serving only as a great place for the neighborhood kids

to sneak in and hang. The French Revolution and the growth of the middle class were tough on royalty: the structure of the work market changed, multiplying many times the cost of maintaining a staff to clean and repair *les grands châteaux*. The turmoil of cultural adjustment threw a tremendous number of finely crafted buildings into abandonment. As the transition finishes, these abandoned buildings become rare.

The building in which this fireplace was found was a *pavillon de chasse* (smaller house near a *château* used as a hunting lodge). The roof had fallen; the stairs were giving way under our feet. Yet the once-elegant fireplace stood tall and *cossue* (opulent) in beautiful white Savonnière limestone, covered by years of oil lamp soot and neglect. Careful inspection showed that she was still sound, worthy, and in need of rescue. A team of five strong men worked meticulously over two days to disassemble it, stone by stone, securing it to pallets for the move to the restoration warehouse.

There, other experts went to work. Out came the brushes, soap and water. No harsh chemicals. The secret is elbow grease and perseverance, *centimètre* by *centimètre*, for as many days as it takes. This one had little damage—no missing ornamentation, all stones in good shape. When there is damage, a *sculpteur sur pierre* (expert stone carver) is called in.

TOP RIGHT: When I say I explore the countryside, I mean it. Growing up in the Basque country instilled in me a love of animals and natural landscapes, and to find old things, one goes where they are. On this day, I was on the hunt for marble-to-match for a repair on a fireplace. The best match is always with marble as old as the piece. I must match the color and quality; and try to match the quarry as well, but this is less often possible. Marble resists erosion and weathering well, so storing unfinished slabs outdoors is fine. Here, in this field alongside the horses, I found pieces of Porphyre de Finlande Rouge, *the marble used to build the tomb of Napoléon. It was rare in Napoléon's time and is extremely rare today. It was amazing! BOTTOM RIGHT: The salvaging, restoration and reuse of architectural elements is akin to the American ethic of recycling milk bottles, except more so. With architecture, you are preserving history and culture as well as resources. These columns of bluestone, which is between limestone and marble in strength, supported a balcony for nearly 300 years. They will serve another 300 years, once a designer with vision puts them to work.*

TOP LEFT: *I brought the set of six chairs back from France with me to California and put them in the hands of Walter Loeliger, a talented man who specializes in clocks but who can bring practically anything back to life. For the chairs, I asked him to duplicate the original color.* BOTTOM LEFT: *Fer forgé (forged iron) was a simple adaptation for foundries by the early 1900s. If one traces the development of design, one notices that innovation inches forward; then, when someone conceives a new use, such as "outdoor furniture," suddenly a sub-industry jumps forward, in this case, the spring chair.* TOP RIGHT: *These cast-iron posts, some lamp, some fence, are multihued simply by erosion. None have been painted. Before put into service anew, they will be sandblasted and coated, ready for paint to match their new surroundings.* OPPOSITE: *This giant aluminum alarm clock (more than one foot tall) was made in the 1940s by French clockmaker Blangy. It stopped working about ten years ago. I had my eye on it for a long time and finally was able to wear the guy down and buy it. As soon as it arrives, I will take it to Walter so he can get it working again. Ninety-nine percent of the items I deal with are antique, but occasionally I spot a special newer piece that in another fifty years will be all the more astounding.*

Once cleaned and repaired, the stones are carefully palleted for transport, in this case across an ocean and a continent, to our store in St. Helena, California, where she stands ready for her next habitation.

I spend a third of my time throughout France—searching, investigating, driving, walking—hunting, always for quality only. I go wherever there is hope, to town markets, to auction houses and specialist warehouses, out into the country to the shops of the old masters and individual homes. It pains me to arrive too late, as I did in Toulouse when demolition had destroyed all but five of the jail cell doors (see page 16). There is so little quality left: I must hurry.

I am fortunate to have built a network of trustworthy colleagues who know what I am looking for and understand my standards. They keep a constant eye, so I now can go to France only three or four times a year to inspect, accept or reject.

Discovery and rescue are twin gratifications—basic, present at the start and the finish. I've discovered that another joy I can count on is seeing the amazing and edifying transformations that clients make.

Lee Caplin and Gita Karasik are an interesting, very American couple—married, but with different names; both artists with careers (Lee, a film producer; Gita, a concert pianist); two individuals with

LEFT: *One colleague hunts for doors only, especially ones with "movement," as seen in these doors found near Lille. A typical set of four used between the* salon *(living room) and the* salle á manger *(dining room) of a* maison de maître *or* hôtel particulier *(large town house), the curves and circle detail of the* imposte *(transom) signify Louis Philippe style. The wood is French cypress.* RIGHT: *To scale the doors for American homes, I had our restoration team remove the Louis Philippe-style imposte. The stately set now stands 9.5 x 6 feet (2,8 m high x 1,8 m wide) and has been thoroughly cleaned, with new beveled tempered glass installed. (This view is from the reverse side. The safety cushions are still affixed.)*

BELOW: The writing on these doors from une épicerie *invites you to drop in for a sandwich,* un verre de vin du pays *(glass of local wine),* apéritif *or* une tasse de café *(cup of coffee). Now serving as a divider between the living room and kitchen of a newly constructed villa, homeowner Jon Hagstrom decided not to strip and repaint, preferring the warmth of age and history to welcome his guests as the doors did for 120 years in Bordeaux.*

ABOVE: A wonderful solution for smaller spaces is to set French doors into pockets. These are pitchpin *(yellow pine). Found as a set of four, the second pair is mounted elsewhere in the same house. We cleaned and prepared the wood in the restoration warehouse. The glass was fine, original, circa 1870.*

This kitchen, bright and inviting, is built for serious cooking and family activity. Above the French La Cornue stove, the iron fireback stabilizes the freshness of the space with a feel of permanence and a sense of history. Basque farm kitchens, always busy and the center of family bustle, often used open shelves. The access is immediate and practical for active zones. INSET: Cast-iron firebacks were popular, most made in the foundries east of Paris. This one, circa 1750, features Jeune Femme holding a flame and mirror. It is inset into the stucco wall.

busy, active lives who swirl in and through each other's spheres with love and ease.

One goal was to open up their home to the sun and the welcoming climate of the Central Coast of California. French doors are the answer to a multitude of design aims, and Lee and Gita used them excellently in two astonishingly different ways.

To create access for another outdoor room, they wanted light and privacy. Well, beauty, too, of course. A set of art nouveau doors removed intact from a remodeled home in Brussels worked beautifully. The beveled *verre givré* (frosted glass) and quality brass hardware were still totally sound. In traditional art nouveau style, it was heavily varnished wood. We stripped the varnish down to the bare *pitchpin* (yellow pine). Lee and Gita opened the wall, built a jamb, installed and painted the doors, and, *voilà!*— 9 x 8 feet (2,75 *m* x 2,4 *m*) of access, light and beauty.

For another wall opening onto the garden and pool, the stately, clean lines of four pairs of French doors, crisp in white with clear glass, work beautifully.

Not everyone has the *panache* to design an everyday walk through an art deco door from the master bath into a bedroom with a Napoléon III fireplace. Even though

ABOVE: The art nouveau *movement began at the Paris exposition in 1889, when graceful new designs by Emile Gallé caught the popular imagination. Gallé credited his inspiration to admiration of shapes he found in nature: the curves of a woman, the graceful arcs in the stems and leaves of roses, the sweep of a dragonfly in flight. This led to "movement" in designs being recognized.* OPPOSITE TOP: *This seventeenth-century well is a* monolithe *(the basin carved from one stone) and would have been found in front of a* maison de maître. *The mottled, coarse limestone was quarried near Vallée de la Dordogne. The hand crank is missing, but in other respects, the piece is excellent.* OPPOSITE BOTTOM: *The white marble fireplace with the bronze* couronne *(crown) and* pomme de pin *(pinecone) ornamentation signify Empire period. The darkest one is Louis Philippe. The color of the marble has no relation to the style. A tight crystal forms marble. This is the virtue and the bane of the stone. It means that marble can be polished to a brilliance, but it also will break easily if hit at a certain angle. Both of the Caplin fireplaces (pages 60 and 61) were standing like these, as a collection of disjointed, undignified pieces of possibility, in the warehouse of a marble specialist, until need and vision rescued them.*

the time spans for the periods cross, the physical feel is disparate. Gita Karasik's influence—her love of clean lines, orderliness and Eastern serenity—created specific space for each piece, with no sense of clash or conflict.

While serving in France as the U. S. diplomatic representative prior to the French Revolution, Thomas Jefferson came to admire many aspects of French life and culture. His

OPPOSITE: *French doors always have divided lights at least two-thirds of their distance. They became popular after the Industrial Revolution, when demand for workers filled the cities with town houses, or* hôtels particuliers. *Because these new structures had no side views, light entered only from the front to back. Doors that allowed light to travel unimpeded became so desirable that the added expense of craftsmanship fell to inconsequence.*

LES ÉPOQUES ET LES STYLES

XIIIe - XIVe - XVe
13th, 14th, 15th Centuries

HAUTE ÉPOQUE GOTHIQUE

XVIe
16th Century

RENAISSANCE

François Ier	*Henri II*
(1515-1547)	(1547-1559)

XVIIe
17th Century

Louis XIII		*Louis XIV*
Henri IV (1589-1610)	Louis XIII (1610-1643)	Louis XIV (1643-1715)

XVIIIe
18th Century

Régence	*Louis XV*	*Louis XVI*	*Directoire*
Régence (1715-1723)	Louis XV (1723-1774)	Louis XVI (1774-1793)	Révolution (1793-1795) Directoire (1795-1799) Consulat (1799-1804)

XIXe
19th Century

Empire	*Restauration*	*Louis Phillipe*	*Napoléon III*
Empire (1804-1815)	Louis XVIII (1815-1824)	Charles X (1824-1830) Louis Phillipe (1830-1848)	IIeme République (1848-1852) Napoléon III (1852-1870)

XXe
20th Century

Style 1900

Modern Style or Art Nouveau
Art Deco
(1871-1950)

LEFT: *Detailed exquisitely, as art deco requires, this master bath is a stunner. An embroidered Jan de Luz bath towel hangs on the* cuvette *(basin).*
OPPOSITE: *This Napoléon III fireplace is white Italian marble with encrustation of golden-veined Italian marble. Additional white marble was carefully matched to fill in the firebox to the size of the modern gas log inset. The sleigh bed is Louis Philippe–influenced, with its gently curved side and soft edges.*

LEFT: *Of the three periods of Napoléon-style furnishings, Napoléon III is the most popular for fireplaces. On a Napoléon III, you will find ornamentation in copper, shell, stone or other durable materials affixed to the* base de la tablette *and* jambage. *Here, in the Caplin-Karasik living room, a Napoléon III of black marble from Italy is inlaid with a second, well-veined marble. The lines are clean and sweet, with a formal delicacy that make Napoléon III fireplaces particularly well suited for American libraries and bedrooms. The Buddha atop the fireplace is a perfect complement.*

ABOVE: Back when self-sufficiency was a need as well as a value, French landowners, petits and grands, made wine from grapes grown on their property. As natural as curing milk into cheese, making wine has been a mainstay of French life since, especially, the 1600s. Every property needed a convenient way to dry old wine bottles being cleaned for reuse. Popular today as kitchenware, bottle-drying racks are thus being preserved. RIGHT: The French Touch exemplifies la joie de vivre. Begin with a willingness to combine eclectic elements as expression of your spirit. Spit aside the old idea of toeing the ligne de rigueur. Here, a champagne-turning rack adds frivolity and its echo of the past to a sunny California porch.

experiences in France reinforced his understanding that context is important, insisting that one's surroundings affect a person in a way similar to thoughts. Choose wisely, he cautioned, for what we choose to keep around us becomes a "museum of our soul and the archives of our experience." Lee and Gita understand and agree with this Jeffersonian sentiment.

The heart of my work is in locating authentic pieces and getting them in position to assume renewed purpose. Most often, the elements serve again as they did originally—a mantel from a Paris *hôtel particulier* becoming, say, a bedroom fireplace in Peoria.

These tiles from Gironde were made from local clay the old-fashioned way— across the thigh of the worker. To create sufficient quantity in coordinated colors for a new construction, I carefully matched pieces from the roofs of perhaps a half-dozen demolished homes.

Other times, a new purpose emerges—such as stone pillars that once supported a Lille balcony now installed to define the transition from kitchen to family room. I have no prejudice between same use or new purpose. The more practical the better, and the more innovative the better. Innovation and practicality are not mutually exclusive. It's true that Eduardo Venegas's daring strut of installing a spiral staircase that goes nowhere (other than into the heart of everyone who experiences its delight) is uncommon, but many transformed uses are wonder-

fully practical—a roofing tile used as a drain, a bottle rack as a glass rack, old roofing tiles sorted and compiled to assemble new options, a Louis XIII mantel used as a range hood.

I don't even mind when someone mistakes upside-down, if they are thoughtful and choosing independently, not just being cavalier. When I arrived to inspect an installation of a Louis XV limestone fireplace in a remodel, I saw the contractor had installed the legs upside down. This looked terribly awkward to me (well, backward, actually), but the client liked them that way, and so they stay. Similarly, another client likes her Louis XVI *frise* with *des nœuds de ruban* (garland of ribbon and bows) upside down. Fine.

OPPOSITE: *The limestone in this Régence-style surround has been "aged" by application of a special* tisane *made from oak leaves. The goal was to bring the stone from its natural pale blonde to a complementary color between the ochre of the stucco and the sand of the paving stone. The walnut door echoes influences from the south of France in the strong bolts for the hinges and the square center beveled moldings.*
LEFT: *This* frise *in the style of Louis XVI (identifiable by the line of nœuds de ruban [garland of ribbon and bows]), upside-down, conveys a surprising Oriental feel.*

I am not a purist; I am a passionist. I say, know what you like and why, and then act on it, responsibly. In matters of decoration, if some arbitrary rules are broken, a new one will be coming along.

I also find joy in creating new pieces. Working with quality materials and true craftsmen is exciting, and challenges presented by homeowners, designers and architects are fun. For example, Greg Blackwell, a competent and resourceful professional builder, brought us his original designs. He had particular details in mind. It was more straightforward to craft them for him than to hunt down pieces that would satisfy. I know

from my own design experience, when someone is burning with ideas, one wants self-expression. Ideas in the head are one thing. Ideas on paper are a step better, but no seriously creative person will be satisfied until the designs reach full form, whether that be in stone,

Finally, it's a pity, but the rarest finds are often associated with tragedy. When an earthquake hit the south of France about ten years ago, a small village church crumbled, along with much else. I was in the region on a regular buying trip when a friend tipped me to a very special rescue mission.

The church had decided not to try to rebuild, and in order to raise money to help the village recover, the church was selling whatever items it could salvage. This was exciting for me. Awful, too, of course. To have misfortune be a part of the reason fine things become available is tragic, but so are the consequences of people being blind to their own history. An earthquake is a fast-occurring tragedy that can be seen. Cultural ignorance and apathy are hidden diseases, ones which act slowly but inexorably, and are no less tragic.

Thus, the circumstances of the earthquake were unfortunate, and I wanted to help if I could; was glad to be able to do so right away. It is satisfying to help so directly. I purchased all the clerical pieces not destroyed by the earthquake—a double confessional, several pews, the *chaire* (rostrum) and *autel d'église* (curate's table).

It was a good day. As is this day.

> TO HAVE MISFORTUNE BE A PART OF THE REASON FINE THINGS BECOME AVAILABLE IS TRAGIC, BUT SO ARE THE CONSEQUENCES OF PEOPLE BEING BLIND TO THEIR OWN HISTORY.

Is there a more striking adaptation of a fireplace mantel? The simplicity of the line of Louis XIII makes this style especially easy to use in many décors. OVERLEAF: The collapse of the church roof damaged the door and the cross on the chapiteau, *and the aged* chêne *(oak) was cloaked in stone dust. Gentle restoration experts repaired the damage, cleaned and waxed all surfaces many times with lavender beeswax. Today, the confessional adds distinction to the foyer of a new home at Santa Lucia Preserve. The inscription above the door reads "M. le 2ème Vicaire" (second vicar, assistant to the curate).*

DISCOVERING PASSION

IN THE AMERICAN WAY OF SAYING THINGS FAST: FASHION FADES; STYLE STICKS. FASHION COMES THROUGH PURPORTED ADVICE FROM MAGAZINES AND CRITICS; SOMETHING YOU ADOPT. STYLE, THOUGH, ISN'T SOMETHING THAT YOU APPLY LIKE HAND CREAM. IT COMES FROM WITHIN, AS AN EMANATION FROM YOUR OWN BEING. IF IT SEEMS A BIT DEVILISH, MAYBE IT HAS TO BE TO CAPTURE RIGHTLY THE WHOLE YOU. There is a romantic fantasy persisting in America, or at least in the *idea* of America: that of chasing the sunset into a new life with the promise of renewal through new effort. In a way, I am a poster child for good sec-

This cast-iron staircase, made around 1900, is a fine example of late fonte d'art. *The advances in foundry technology permitted circular staircases to be designed for easy on-site assembly from factory-made parts, making them one of the first "modular component designs." Typical of the style made in northern France, I found this staircase in a private home in Lille. The staircase will soon be installed in a busy family home on the East Coast.*

Amour au Papillon *(front)*, *by Canova*, Faune Flûteur, *and* Bacchus *are three statues representative of the decorative art that became popular after M. Victor André made innovations in casting iron at the Val d'Osne Foundry near Marne. Each is mounted on a different limestone pedestal chosen to complement the individual piece. They stand in front of a well reproduced to my design, featuring two monolithe columns quarried in the south of France. The well supplies water for a grove of 320 olive trees.*

ond chapters in life. Our transition to living in America has been relatively easy; and I am quick to admit gratitude. Still, my brand of realism suggests the goal is to be cheery, not necessarily happy. One can—nay, one *must*—find contentment in how the day plays out, even when perfection is, as usual, a no-show.

This is one reason why I enjoy interaction with people as they make major transitions in their living spaces. Humans are perpetually confronting or constructing turning points; and major changes in living space always indicate transitions are happening. The ones I witness are transitions that people have chosen for themselves. It is exciting, and a totally human event. Whether you are packing the crates for a move to a new country, unfurling the blueprints for a new house you designed yourself or had designed, or simply changing the mantel art, change always indicates a point of attention, and what we focus on changes us. As the American poet John Ciardi said, "A man is what he does with his attention."

Today's speed of communication, the nearly instantaneous transfer of impressions, pushes change into individuals and cultures faster than ever. Humankind's ease toward distraction and ricocheting emotions becomes a problem. Neither individuals nor nations absorb change beyond some natural limit. This, in part, is why founding the *éco-musée* for Basque traditions meant so much to me, and why I have a passion for rescuing fine

> KEEPING CULTURAL HISTORY ALIVE SLOWS THE ABSORPTION OF CHANGE. PAUSING TO REFLECT IS A NATURAL TONIC.

pieces of old architecture. Keeping cultural history alive slows the absorption of change. Pausing to reflect is a natural tonic. Whether stressed by duties or manic with the excitement of designing, I try to remind myself to pause, to not hurry so fast from task to task. The hour can get so cluttered with the details of the moment or the goal of the day that life itself gets buried. This is a form of demolition as surely as taking a wrecking ball to a thirteenth-century stone building.

Long a passion of mine has been Val d'Osne sculptures. The history of this once great foundry that disappeared is illustrative of my general point—that change is, at its most elemental, a point of attention.

The Haute-Marne valley in Champagne-Ardenne, east of Paris, had produced iron for twenty-five centuries. Europe's earliest iron implements—swords and horse bits, generally—are from Marne ore. With the best iron ore in France, and the other two necessities—wood to fuel the furnaces and year-round rivers with sufficient force to provide power—the Marne became home to a dozen foundries and crowned the metallurgic

OPPOSITE: The process of fonte d'art *begins with a stone or wooden model. As here, for* Faune Flûteur, *sculptors prefer fine-grained hardwoods because they can carve more detail. Wood always carries finer detail than any stone model, even ones carved in the smoothest marble. The model is used to form a shape in uniformly fine, properly dampened and well-tamped sand or clay, creating a mold. After preparing the surface of the mold and spraying it with alcohol, specially formulated smelted iron is poured into the mold, which is closed (a process requiring the right tools and skill) and cooled. When fully hardened, the mold is opened, the sculpture removed and cleaned and the edges sanded to remove any burrs.*

capital of Europe when the royal order for 400 firebacks and pipe for the fountains for Versailles arrived in 1681.

Through the ensuing 200 years, the Marne continued as one of France's most productive industrial regions, and then in one quick decade, it became the center of a wholly new art form. It is another of history's small stories that confirm that one passionate person acting responsibly and with persistence can transform an industry and change the world. This man was Jean-Pierre Victor André.

In 1833, André was manager of the Brousseval and Thonnance-les-Joinville ironworks in the Marne. He had ideas about how to expand the business, but management wasn't listening. To break tradition, he needed to be his own boss; so, on October 28, 1834, he petitioned King Louis Philippe for authorization to build his own smelting furnace at a former priory hidden in a small valley, the Val d'Osne.

Everyone thought his choice of location was odd. The Osne was a mere stream, not a full-fledged river. Would he have enough power? Why did he choose being so far away from the main commerce roads? Only later did his thinking make sense to others, when they realized that what he wanted was Val d'Osne's convenient source of sand.

Finally, on April 5, 1836, the royal edict

ABOVE: Perhaps it will surprise you to learn that only the posts are fonte. *Cast between 1850 and 1860 as part of a huge order for the fences along Belgium canals, now the posts create smiles and a convenient resting spot at the edge of José Desmet's koi pond (which is complete with mirrors for the fish). The tractor seats, of stamped iron, are a modern American classic—John Deere!* OPPOSITE: *Only the* jardinière *(planter) is* fonte d'art. *The candlestick and the iron table base are* fer forgé *(wrought iron).*

came through. André was in business as the Val d'Osne Foundry. He started up with all the usual complement of utilitarian products—pipes, manhole covers, firebacks, cooking pots. The most decorative product was the occasional plaque (see page 19; this one in brass, rather than iron), but he started experimenting with ores and methods and started tapping the skills of sculptors. André was living in Paris, which, in those

BELOW: This table de boucherie *(display table for meats from a delicatessen), always marble-topped because marble stays cold, is an elegant 6 x 3 feet (1,80 m long x 0.9 m wide). The* fonte d'art tulipe *and* pomme de pin *(pine cone) design, presented upside-down, is late-19th century. The legs are* fer forgé *and brass. Two cast-iron vases and a* fonte d'art *bird cage sit among Chinese monkeys and ginger jars. OPPOSITE: Once the idea of ornamental iron took hold, functional outdoor pieces were among the first to be adapted. This settee, in the Rancho Santa Fe garden of Jim and Mary Beth Crowley, was cast in three sections, the back and arms, the seat, and the legs, which were then assembled at the foundry with nuts and bolts. This design of grapes and leaves was enormously popular, and similar designs are still being made today.*

years on the front edge of the Industrial Revolution, was prowling with artists. André easily found sculptors willing to design decorative gates, fences, balcony and stair rails, chandeliers, fountains, statuary and religious icons and accoutrements. No one had conceived of using iron to make something pretty. Beauty was the preserve of marble and bronze, but

iron? Not until André. And once Val d'Osne started producing items that were also beautiful, his small foundry went from one cupola (furnace) run by André and a couple workers to adding two more cupolas and employing 220 ironmasters by 1844. In just eight years, his new art form was a worldwide sensation.

Paris was abuzz. People in the industry acknowledged that André knew the smelt-

ing business, but criticized that he had no training in art. What he was doing was inconceivable, but he did it. He knew what he liked and went after it with a passion, watching the quality.

André's passion took smelting from industrial utility into the first union of art and industry, a world mania known as *"fonte d'art."* Unfortunately, he barely had a chance to realize what a success his inspiration became. He didn't live to see Val d'Osne win major prizes at *L'exposition universelle* in Paris in 1855 (and at succeeding major exhibitions) or see a mania for his new art form circle the globe, distributing the work of sixteen French sculptors through thirty-three countries. He died, while working at the foundry in 1851.

Travelers can spot actual Val d'Osne pieces or their influence throughout Europe and Russia, particularly St. Petersburg; from Soho (both London and New York); throughout the French Quarter in New Orleans and the interior of the Bradley Building in Los Angeles; and the public squares of Rio de Janeiro especially, which, because

Above: Nymph Daphnis (Daphne) sits sweetly playing the flute, draped in sheep's skin with a front hoof still attached. Soon, Apollo will come a-chasing. To protect herself, Daphnis will transform herself into laurel, or so goes the story.

it missed the ravages of two World Wars, is a virtual open-air museum of nineteenth-century statuary art.

We no longer know the names of the first sculptors who helped André with the design work, but the first to become famous was Mathurin Moreau, whose fountains, monuments and sculptures, particularly in Rio, monopolize art history and catalogs of the period. Moreau designs are classical, but elegant and refined. His delicacy in rendering the female form helped advance the art world from classical to art nouveau. Understandably, Moreau's cast-iron pieces produced at Val d'Osne are prized, but he also worked in plaster, marble, bronze and silver. A one-time administrator of Val d'Osne after André's death, Moreau had an interest in technical innovations and even took a civic turn, becoming *maire* (mayor) of the nineteenth *arrondissement* (district) of Paris. Moreau died at age ninety, holder of more medals from world exhibitions than anyone in history.

After André's death, his wife managed Val d'Osne for several years before selling to Gustave Barbezat, a protégé of André who continued the foundry's expansion and proved to be a conscientious employer by establishing France's first employee housing in 1866. After Barbezat, Val d'Osne passed through a series of corporate hands as it continued to be the world master in art casting. The years 1870 to 1892 were especially productive.

Wars are disruptive, of course. Workers' logs for 1917 show the main production shifted to grenades and shells, once the French government commandeered the foundry as a national resource during the turmoil of WWI.

OPPOSITE: *It's generally agreed that France's iconic* tour Eiffel *would not have been accepted had André not transformed iron into ornamental works of every imagination fifty years earlier. Designed by engineer Alexandre Gustave Eiffel and erected between January 28, 1887 and March 31, 1889, for the 1889 World's Fair in Paris, which celebrated the centenary of the French Revolution,* tour Eiffel *demonstrated the advances made in iron architecture. It consists of more than 18,000 pieces of iron connected by 2,500,000 rivets, standing 1,059 feet (324 m). There are 1,665 steps to the top.*

In 1931, the Durenne Cie, long the only serious competition for Val d'Osne, bought the foundry and redirected production, maintaining ornamental casting (garden furniture, vases, chandeliers and the like), but phasing out all art casting (statuary and fountains) except religious works.

WWII was even more disruptive than WWI, with many European fountains and statuary being destroyed by bombs or through emergency recycling of anything iron into new armaments. Many Val d'Osne pieces found demise in the same cupolas from which they emerged as art. In the gloomy spirit of those years, most of the plaster models for the art works were broken up and tossed onto the slagheap. Religious respect compelled preserving the models of the religious pieces, in a storage room called "Paradise." The last order the Val d'Osne foundry produced came from the Vatican. Val d'Osne closed in 1986, at a time when museums and art auctions were clamoring for the best *fonte d'art* from the previous century. The best extant examples of Val d'Osne statuary are in the major Catholic churches worldwide, the public squares of Rio de Janeiro, and in museums and private collections.

I started collecting nineteenth-century statuary about twelve years ago. It is a passion, something that comes from deep within; I grew up surrounded by monuments. When I was young, a neighbor had an antiques warehouse. I practically grew up in it, which led to my trading

ABOVE: L'Egyptien *and* Le Nubien *(second from left and right front, respectively) are Mathurin Moreau creations, circa 1850. Standing center front is* L'enfant au poisson *(child with fish), also by Moreau. The lady holding a child on her shoulder, behind the two green* jardinières, *by L. Thiriot (1887), is* Bacchante *(consort of* Bacchus, *in the photograph on pages 72–73), cast to the original marble by Claude Michel (Clodion), which is on permanent display in le Louvre. Standing behind the green* jardinière *on the right side is* La Source à l'enfant, *by Moreau. On the grass at far left is* Jeune Homme, *holding a torch, by Moreau. At right front is a Louis XVI vase.* OPPOSITE: Le chasseur *(hunter), cast at L. Thiriot, is a boy holding his catch, a rabbit, high on his shoulders as his dog tries to jump for it. He stands 6 feet (1,83 m) without the pedestal. I made the pedestal of limestone quarried in Provence.*

antiques as a form of self-employment as a teenager. It is part of what I mean when I say antiquities belong to my blood.

I concentrate on works crafted from 1836 to 1880, but collecting as investment only is paltry soul work. I wouldn't bother unless I loved the individual piece, unless having it actually delighted me, unless it energized something in the soul. Part of the affection comes from knowing André's story, surely, a constant reminder of his passion and, in the American vernacular, his stick-to-it-iveness. When I look at a Val d'Osne, I see beauty, yes, but I am also reminded to get to work!

I hunt for quality, distinctive architectural antiques that are beautiful and still useful but which are about to be knocked to rubble by demolition, are sitting buried in the basements of auction houses, or are lost in overstuffed rooms where more-for-more's-sake is mistaken for merit. Admittedly, merit is an abstract. It has no intrinsic value, only the illusion of value we humans ascribe to it, and this illusion wavers according to time and circumstance, as personality and taste do. Whatever the craze—leather-bound first editions, gold, nineteenth-century *fonte d'art* or even tulips—everyone agrees there is *some* value; the question is how much— and that depends on the nature of human distraction.

We really can embarrass ourselves with our distractions, can't we? One by one, we can seduce ourselves with needs and greeds. A person can be a wit one day, a nitwit the next. And crazes are infectious. So many people can acquire a new habit in such a short time that national, even global, franchises sprout. Take Starbucks. The pleasure of espresso became a new daily rite for so many—for

RIGHT: Le Petit Chaperon Rouge (Little Red Riding Hood), created by Anna Latry in 1889 and cast at Fonderie du Salin, a Val d'Osne competitor, is one of the premier examples of fonte d'art because of its charming proportions and sharp detail. It is the second of only two cast iron sculptures by Latry. The first, Cendrillon (Cinderella) was created in 1888.

some a new "right"—that the franchise is ubiquitous in America and fast going worldwide. People acquire habits while ignoring that the independence of personal savings is an actual need. Such is the power of distraction. Whole nations are seducible—for tulips or gold or dot-com bubbles—whenever imagination promotes desire to the status of need. It's a form of insanity—the fantasy part of the psyche overwhelming the reasoning part.

The market for Val d'Osne fluctuates within a narrow range, generally trending upward, but doesn't tumble wildly. I have to expect it to vary, for all collectibles do, even gold, when world turmoil builds to a fever pitch and the power of hope drains away, supplanted by fear. In such times, everyone finally sees that money is only an instruction, a communication requiring a transmitter and a receiver. If no one is listening, there is no communication, no matter how loud the yell. Turmoil can reduce kings to beheaded legends, and make fat wallets less valuable than a laborer's skilled hands. Money is a currency, temporal; a collectible with a value that varies according to human attention.

This is why I collect only artifacts that I love. Quality is essential. Only quality is beautiful and soul-enriching; only quality survives the transitory nature of human distraction.

HEARTH AS HOME

HUMANKIND CAPTURED FIRE FOR WARMTH, LEARNED TO COOK, SMELT AND FORGE, AND, IN EVER MORE AUGMENTING WAYS, LED A BETTER LIFE. WHETHER HUDDLED IN A CAVE OR ON THE ROAM AS A HUNTER-GATHERER, LIFE AROUND A FIRE STRENGTHENED TRIBAL BONDS AND IMPROVED ODDS FOR SURVIVAL. LIFE WAS EASIER IN THE EXPECTED WAYS OF WARMTH AND FOOD, AND THEN IN OTHER WAYS AS WELL—ANOTHER OF THOSE INTERCONNECTIONS THAT MAKE LIFE DURABLE AND FASCINATING. ᏒᎧ The Basque country of southwestern France is beautiful, and wet. The western Pyrenees, averaging 10,000 feet (3,400 *mètres*) catch moisture flying in from the Atlantic and pull it out of the sky. The Pyrenees boast more spectacular *cascades* (waterfalls) than anywhere in Europe other

The harmony of a wooden fireplace and paneling in the welcoming library in the home of Jim and Mary Beth Crowley in Rancho Santa Fe, California, is enlivened by print fabrics, a sparkling crystal chandelier and Louis XV cor de chasse sconces.

BELOW: A Louis XV as it stood in the warehouse. The pink color is an illusion: the elegantly smooth Poitiers-region limestone is reflecting the color of the wall. The limestone is actually pale blonde. OPPOSITE: The gradation of the color of the limestone in the trumeau is natural. A talented compagnon *(workman) would trouble himself to include a pleasant variation of color in the stone as he is crafting a* cheminée. *Often homeowners initially question the harmony of the different colors, but invariably, once installed and seen in the new natural setting, the original character becomes loved. This one, circa 1920, is from the region of Nancy.*

than in the high country of Scandinavia. (The highest in the Pyrenees is at Cirque de Gavarnie, which falls a beautiful 1,515 feet [461 *m*], at the head of the Gave de Pau.)

Sensibly, Basque houses have always had fireplaces. It doesn't matter that modern thermal science can provide comfort by means of what in America is called central heating. No Basque house would forfeit the heritage and conviviality of a fireplace. Simplicity has merit, but reductionism does not. If the simpler ways erase the texture and context that make a life, a family, and a home strong, then you have oversimplified.

When I was a boy, we still cooked in the fireplace, which meant the fireplace was in the kitchen, the hub of home—the place where you dried your boots coming in from chores, washed your hands, sat around the *table de ferme* (long table) talking and eating a little bread warmed over the fire. There was always a pot of soup or stock simmering in the *crémaillère* (hanging iron pot for fireplace use).

In September, my father, brother and I would go to the section of the forest assigned to our family and cut wood for the winter. We would work eight or ten days during the month—long, hard days—cutting and splitting ten to twelve *stères* of wood

Louis XV Ref: K18053
W 63 X H 60 X D 25

W 65 X H 112 X D 18

Ref: K18014

OVERLEAF: *Comfortable sofas now sit in front of the Louis XV fireplace, making it a favorite place for the family to gather several times a day. This is the Basque spirit of togetherness. The mason, Richie DeAmaral, built the firebox in split herringbone and to true Count Rumford dimensions—shallower with widely angled covings and a rounded, streamlined throat—to improve draft and increase the amount of heat radiated forward. Count Rumford, the first person to understand that heat is a form of motion and who defined engineering as the "application of science to the common purposes of life," also devised the first drip coffeemaker. The pots on the mantel are traditional* pots de confit *from the Basque region of southwestern France, used to store prepared pig, goose or duck through the winter. To make a* confit, *braise the meat or fowl in a* crémaillère *over a low fire for several hours until fully cooked. While still hot, arrange the tender pieces of meat tightly in the* pot de confit, *then cover completely with fat rendered from the cooking process, to protect against spoilage by preventing air from entering. Cover the pot with paper and tie with a string or ribbon.*

(about forty cords). A Basque house is designed with wood storage vaults on either side of the front door. It is basic survival: hearth as home, for warmth, togetherness and nourishment—tummy and soul.

The American understanding of fireplaces is more like newer areas of Europe, with rustic hearths in kitchens, tall fireplaces in living rooms or parlors and smaller fireplaces in bedrooms. American homes have efficient heating systems, of course, but no heating system transmits the emotional, sensuous, soul-touching warmth of a live fire. I can't think of any new-construction customer who hasn't chosen a mantel for one or several fireplaces.

Adding the substance and character of an ancient fireplace is a straightforward task these days. With a little planning, it is as simple as building a fireplace with new refractory brick. The trick is to select your mantel before completing the plans, so your architect and contractor will know the size needed for the firebox. Or, if the choice is for a big Gothique or Renaissance *cheminée*, the practical approach may be to set the fireplace early and finish the room around it. Firebox sizes range from 7 feet wide x 8 feet high x 4 feet deep (2 *m* wide x 2,4 *m* high x 1,2 *m* deep), for the largest

ABOVE: A traditional Basque farmhouse is commodious, intended to welcome an active farm family life. The trim is traditionally basque red or basque green, always on white stucco walls. The "trim" is actually structural, load-bearing timbers. (Photo by Jacques Denarnaud)
OPPOSITE: The firebox is outfitted American-fashion with natural gas, completed with on-off key to the left of the jambage. Originally, the corniche of the trumeau would have fit between the beams. Here, in a taller room, the detail of the corniche becomes another graceful line. The wooden baromètre-thermomètre in feuilles d'or (gold leaf) fits beautifully on the mantel.

RIGHT: *The beauty of this Napoléon III fireplace was ignored when modernization to steam radiators swept through this* Ghent maison de maître, *probably after the war. I was able to purchase this one when the interior of the four-story building was being demolished from roof to basement to be remade into condominiums.* BELOW: *Because there were no holes drilled into the marble or other severe damage done to the* cheminée *during the post-WWII modernization, all we had to do to "restore" her was give her a thorough "toothbrush cleaning" with sudsy mild soap and water.* OPPOSITE: *This fine Italian black marble was carved, then painted with* feuilles d'or *(gold leaf). The lion's head is a tribute to the Belgian king, with hunting dogs present for good luck.*

A CASCADE OF FACTORS SETS THE PRICE FOR FIREPLACES. THE FIRST IS RARITY, OF COURSE; THEN THE DEMAND FOR A PARTICULAR STYLE; THEN QUALITY WITHIN THAT STYLE....

Gothique and Renaissance fireplaces capable of cooking for a family, to 4 feet wide x 3 feet high x 2 feet deep (1,2 *m* wide x .9 *m* high x .6 *m* deep) for small ones used for warming bedrooms. Weights range from a few hundred pounds to more than ten tons.

Whatever the size, the choice of stone for an authentic *cheminée* will be limestone or marble, with only a few exceptions. For each stone, there is a wide range of color and texture to consider. Limestone ranges in color and texture, depending on the quarry, from almost pure white and fine-grained through every gradation of ochre to sand, and through shades of pale blue to almost black, and from smooth coloration to wildly mottled. Marble ranges from almost pure white to intense black but is also found in colors—pink, green, brown and beige principally—and with wide variations in degree of veining.

Generally, the *tailleur de pierre* (stonecutter) cut whatever serviceable stone was nearby. Thus, for the majority of authentic mantels, the color and texture of the stone will indicate the general area where the fireplace was crafted. Truly fantastic creations may be found hundreds or even thousands of miles from the source of their stone, but only when the original owner could afford to pay the freight of men transporting heavy stone, block by block, over the distance.

Today, a cascade of factors sets the price of fireplaces. The first is rarity, of course; then the degree of demand for a particular style; then quality within that style (unmarred, all accoutrements included); the quality of the stone within that style; and, finally, the aesthetics of the particular piece (graceful proportions, precise details). Not all *tailleurs de pierre* or *com-*

pagnons (workmen) had the same eye for artistic detail or the patience needed for fine work.

The best sculptors made the best pieces, of course, usually for the rich and titled. Itinerant *compagnons* built most of the fireplaces for modest farmhouses. These *compagnons* would stay out on the road for a year or two at a time, finding any work they could within a few hundred miles from their homes. The quality of the workmanship depended on the individual craftsman. Only a few of the finest *compagnons* signed their work (carved their initials or a signifying mark), so when inspecting a *cheminée* before dismantling it for recovery, you have to know what to look for to judge quality of stone and workmanship, and inspect carefully for soundness.

From back to front, a tall, columned, stone Napoléon III; a barely seen Louis XV; a typically proportion ochre Louis XV with barre de chocolat carving on the linteau; a rimmed, pale limestone Louis XIV; a Régence with its relaxed, curvaceous detail.

With the start of the Industrial Revolution, the demand for housing exploded. New forms of manufacturing centralized work, shifting populations from farms to villages and burgeoning cities. The population shift created the need for new compact housing structures—*maisons de maître* in the country and *hôtels particuliers* (town houses) in the cities—and every living space needed a fireplace for warmth. The tremendous increase in building between 1840 and 1900 meant some craftsmanship would be great, some shoddy. This surge in building created the inventory from which I find authentic mantels today.

The supply is dwindling. The building surge caused by the

ABOVE: The 500 years between the 1472 Gothique fireplace and the 1980s "bones" of this house become inconsequential when design harmonizes color, scale and purpose. The fireplace in the dining room at the rear is a deep-mantled Louis XIII.

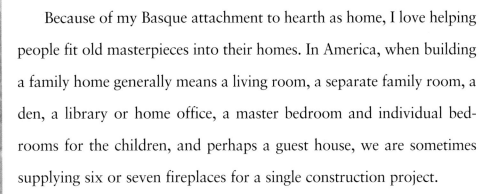

Industrial Revolution led to the destruction of many pre-1800 buildings. Then, after World War II, another great rehabbing occurred throughout Europe, destroying many of the buildings built between 1850 and 1900, either by the war or by modernization. As a salvager, I am in a fight against time to find the best of the remaining few.

Because of my Basque attachment to hearth as home, I love helping people fit old masterpieces into their homes. In America, when building a family home generally means a living room, a separate family room, a den, a library or home office, a master bedroom and individual bedrooms for the children, and perhaps a guest house, we are sometimes supplying six or seven fireplaces for a single construction project.

Working with the parents of a vibrant, growing family became a happy task. They arrived one day, the wife carrying a collection of photographs culled from magazines. They had done their homework. They knew what they liked and just needed help matching preferences for style to the best quality available. They served as their own general contractor, even though neither had training as such. This is

ABOVE: The craftsman's mark etched dead center on the linteau—*MCDLXXII (1472)—was covered for a few centuries by a coat of arms. The homeowners and their designer, Michael Bolton, all agreed with us that it is better not to hide or try to disguise history.*
LEFT: Gothique fireplaces are large and of the strongest stone; generally fairly plain. Here well-carved and finished stones are subtly enhanced by a simple flourish of a single curve. Many Gothique pieces feature a cross or other echoes of religion.

another of those wonderful aspects of freedom in America. If you set your mind to something and accept responsibility, you can step up and do for yourself most of what you intend. They had a normal amount of apprehension, but were always excited and had enough common sense to listen for advice that would steer them around problems. Their confidence and energy allowed them to be both practical and inventive.

We provided roofing tiles from Bordeaux, an eighteenth-century fireback for the La Cornue range in the kitchen (seen on pages 54–55), the front door and surround, a fountain for the garden and five fireplaces, all Louis XVs. For the kitchen (seen on pages 88–89), we chose a medium-size fireplace with long *jambage* (legs), without *trumeau* (portion above the mantel, part of the flue), in an exquisitely smooth limestone from the Poitiers region. The understated design, the paneled *linteau* (mantel) and curve along the *jambage* make it transitional between Louis XIV and Louis XV. In the living room, the installation of another Louis XV with *trumeau* was as straightforward. Their mason, Rich DeAmaral, built the fireboxes, and we built the limestone hearths.

RIGHT: Following Gothique, the Louis XIII period is marked by simplicity of design and elegance of line. This one, in pale, smooth Savonnière limestone, was expertly joined between linteau *and* corbeau *(side piece) with clay by mason Ray Marzorini, who also built the firebox. We matched a piece of raw limestone to form the simple and simply beautiful hearth.*
OPPOSITE: A gnomic devil sits on the linteau *of this Louis XIII, next to a* jardinière *bursting with orchids. The high arms and sweeping curve of the settee signify Louis Philippe.*

For Jon Hagstrom's La Villa Dulce in Carmel, we shifted back in time about two hundred years, from Louis XV to Renaissance, for the elegant and massive fireplace now featured in his living room and on the cover of this book. His designer, Michael Bolton, has a terrifically keen eye. He saw the beauty in her bulk as she stood in the storeroom on her pallet a year or so before a project came along where she would be workable, but he remembered.

When I say that knowing what you like is important and bringing pictures of your preferences is a good idea, it is because the choices are many. On any given day, the choice would be from between 120 and 150 fireplaces; hundreds more if we put out feelers for a special order. Do you want the palest limestone or the blackest marble? Do you want an elegantly detailed Napoléon III; a stately and imposing Louis XV with *barre de chocolat* carving; a plumply rimmed Louis XIV; or a narrow, brown marble Régence?

Another Michael Bolton success story is the redesign of a well-built but dated home constructed in the 1980s. The new owners wanted to lose some of the coolness of the Modern atmosphere and bring it forward into a significant and singular expression just for themselves. To "bring it forward," they added something very old—a

Louis XIV fireplaces always have a prominent "brow" on the front edge of the mantel, and generally have deep carving. On this trumeau, *two* colonnes (columns) surmount the chapiteaux ioniques, *and a* frise de cubes reliant *(attached to) the* corniche.

pièce de résistance gothique from 1472 (seen on pages 98–99). Small for a Gothique, Michael lifted it off the floor with a new stone *piètement.* Comfortable seating in front of the hearth takes advantage of the warmth.

To add liveliness and to marry purpose and aesthetics invisibly, Michael added two other fireplaces to the home.

A small and graceful Louis XIII fits beautifully in the adjoining dining room. In the master bedroom, a small Louis XIII adds warmth and *présence* without intruding (seen on pages 100–101).

Richard Wax, a man of incredible energy and spirit with a fantastically busy life, wanted a strong, masculine feel for his living room in Napa Valley. He chose a highly carved white-and-grey limestone Louis XIV with *trumeau* that is assertive from every angle. It defines the room. Richard designed the new hearth of flat-gray and blue-gray limestone, and added a stone inset above the *corniche* (topmost portion with horizontal designs) of the *trumeau* integrated with the flue, which adds steadiness to the structure.

I've learned that there is always a difference between people, and that the natures of people are not altogether gender based. A woman can be as decisive as a man can be, while some men can be as meek as some women are. Tastes and temperaments vary tremendously, within both genders as much as among age and cultural groups. There are differences always: you have to meet people where they are, and see them as who they have chosen to be.

I met Nancy (Mrs. Norman) Nason of Saratoga, California, soon after we opened the Carmel store. She knew what she liked and was decisive, selecting a small wooden French mantel for their bedroom. Several years later, when the Carmel Valley store opened, she again arrived knowing what she was looking for, and chose a marble Louis XV with brass *rideau* (screen). Any fireplace as distinctive as this one will surely dominate a room, which is what Mrs. Nason wanted. To ensure it would be the focal point, she painted the surrounding wall a deep blue, so the creamy white marble would "pop."

Friends cried, "You can't do that!" Nancy ignored the faint-hearts. She had a vision. To complement its sophistication and richness, she added a well-proportioned mirror above and ancient Chinese ginger

To realize deep, ornate carving, you must start with marble more than one foot thick. The brass rideau *(screen) itself radiates heat, and features adjustable vents to direct the amount of warmth coming forward. The ornate, highly twined rocailles (designs of stones) on the* rideau *and the marble signify Louis XV.*

jars, flowers and candles on the *linteau*, with refined fabric edged in blue as a "frame," creating a different success from Richard Wax's equally strong statement.

The weather in southern California doesn't necessitate that people warm by the fire very often, certainly less than in other areas of the country; still, busy lives are softened by gathering round a hearth. In the sumptuously detailed Rancho Santa Fe home of Jim and Mary Beth Crowley, fireplaces abound. In the entry, Mary Beth chose a superb Régence with a room-expanding Louis XVI mirror. In the formal living room, she wanted a more sedate Régence to add a dignified presence in a luxurious room. For a bedroom, Mary Beth chose a Louis XV marble fireplace, and dressed it with a Napoléon III clock and *chandeliers* (candlesticks) with *incrustation de porcelaine*. In the formal sitting room, a Régence-style mirror tops a narrow Régence-style fireplace. Finally, in the library, she balanced a sophisticated carved-wood Louis XV–style mantel faced with marble with an appropriate Louis XV mirror.

That's the beautiful thing about style: you make it all your own. The better you know what you like and the more boldly you address yourself to what you like, the more definitive your own expressive style. Mary Beth Crowley conveys her own assured personality in every room, while giving each room a distinct personality.

The next rooms we view are just as sophisticated as Mary Beth's home, but they feel and look worlds apart. At one end of the expansive living room is a Louis XV mantel with *trumeau* that rises high all the way to the beams, with a Louis XV mirror above. At the other end of the room sits an almost twin Louis XV, this time

THE BETTER YOU KNOW WHAT YOU LIKE AND THE MORE BOLDLY YOU ADDRESS YOURSELF TO WHAT YOU LIKE, THE MORE DEFINITIVE YOUR OWN EXPRESSIVE STYLE.

Twin small Louis XV bergères *sit beside this white limestone* Régence *mantel. The mirror is Louis XVI with a* médaillon *painting at the top.*

RIGHT: The gradations of color of the limestone give the mantel a less formal feeling. The floor is Burgundy limestone. The hearth is a single slab of limestone carved to complement the shaping at the linteau. *OPPOSITE: Practically everything you see here is Louis XV, from the mantel to the* alcôve *and* coquille *trim on the bookshelves and door; even the color.*

holding some serious blue porcelain and silver candlesticks. Upstairs, a small and dainty Louis XV without *trumeau* is raised off the floor to provide warmth right at bed level. And in the kitchen (see page 110) presides a simple but impressive Louis XIII with a custom *trumeau* built between the beams.

As a final look at variance of style and purpose, look (on page 111) at the bold Louis XIII *cheminée* in the kitchen of Mike and Kira Whitaker's new home. When they bought the house, they didn't know they had a fireplace close to four hundred years old. Their sons, then four and five years old, could run around inside the firebox intended to handle cooking for a fair-sized estate. I love that Mike didn't want to "tidy up" the rough edges where a flake of limestone had been knocked off.

While Kira isn't interested in homey tradition of *crémaillère* stews, living with the direct warmth of a fireplace in the kitchen has inspired Mike to do a major remodel so they can add a big Renaissance fireplace to their living room and a tall, noble Louis XV with *trumeau* in the master bedroom. While he was

in the store inspecting and choosing I teased Mike that since he has a Renaissance, a Louis XIII and a Louis XV, he could, in American baseball speak, complete the cycle with a small Louis XVI in the master bath.

BELOW: Large enough for family cooking, all this Renaissance fireplace needs is a crémaillère and a few iron cooking pots. OPPOSITE: This Louis XIII mantel is crafted in the excellently tight and fine-grained limestone quarried at le plateau de Langres, in eastern France near Dijon. Above the mantel is a hotte en osier (rattan basket) carried on one's back for harvesting.

It is wonderful to get to know clients and their families well enough to joke with them, and to see how adding the substance of history and the character of time to living spaces helps to unite families. Families are tribal units in the best sense of the word. It seems to me, deeply etched by Basque heritage, that Americans are so busy striving for the latest flavor of success they sometimes forget how important it is to thrive. You cannot be striving and thriving at the same time. And maybe it is not as important to net yet another success as it is to pause and hug your child, kiss your spouse and stay in for dinner, around the fireplace, talking and sharing. Hearth as home is more than a metaphor in Basque tradition.

GARDENS OF
DELIGHT

LEONARDO DA VINCI REGARDED NATURE AS THE SOURCE OF ALL KNOWLEDGE, AS WHERE WE BEGIN TO SORT OUT THE RULES OF THE WORLD, DISCOVERING HOW PLANTS AND ANIMALS GROW AND HOW WE INTEGRATE, FIRST, OUR NEEDS AND, ULTIMATELY, OUR PREFERENCES INTO THE LIMITATIONS AND POSSIBILITIES OF LIFE. THE MOST INVENTIVE MAN OF THE RENAISSANCE, DA VINCI FELT THERE WAS NO EFFECT WITHOUT CAUSE, NO INVENTION WITHOUT PURPOSE. I WANT TO ASK HIM, IS THE SIGHT OF A FLOWER IN BLOOM SUFFICIENT IN PURPOSE TO JUSTIFY MY DELIGHT? THE FLOWER BLOOMS FOR ITSELF, A STEP MERELY NECESSARY FOR ITS SEED TO RIPEN. MY DELIGHT IS NOT WITH THE SEED OR THE PROSPECT OF ANOTHER FLOWER LATER. MY DELIGHT IS SIMPLY WITH THE FLOWER'S BEAUTY NOW. I NEED TO TALK WITH LEONARDO—RIGHT AWAY. ✺ When we chose

continued on page 121

As soon as the weather warms, the French love to eat out-of-doors (manger dehors). *Farmhouses would have an arbor near the house, or a place for a* table de ferme (long table) *under a tree in the orchard. Because the chairs would need to be stored in the winter,* les chaises pliantes (folding chairs) *have been made in France for centuries.*

The 1870 vases are master-pieces of fonte d'art *(see "Discovering Passion" chapter for a history of the movement that legitimatized cast iron as suitable for ornamentation). A classic design of the Empire period, the godrons are tightly scalloped, with large pendants hanging on opposing sides from the mouths of the lions. These pendants are decorative and have no purpose. (They are not handles!). Vases from this period are often embossed with the name of the foundry. Val d'Osne and J. J. Ducel made many, so you might see "J. J. Ducel, Mtre de forge à Paris" as a signature.*

TOP: *Vases such as these would have been placed on pillars near a doorway or in the garden, planted with geraniums.* ABOVE: *Homeowners Jim and Mary Beth Crowley provided this photo, showing a vase identical to those they chose for their pool fountain. The photograph, taken early in the 1900s in the south of France, shows three generations of a French family in a small patio garden. Notice the two* chaises pliantes *(folding chairs), later to be referred to as "French bistro chairs."* RIGHT: *The same fountain seen on the preceding page, from a longer view. Such symmetry is never accidental. At center rear, another fountain.*

LEFT: *This backyard garden includes a lawn, a pool, a Jacuzzi, an allée of climbing roses, a separate bed of hybrid tea roses, perennials, and a pétanque court.* ABOVE: *Pétanque is a lovely family game. The rules, equipment and play are simple, yet the outcome is in doubt until the last* boule *(ball) is tossed. Age, strength and speed are not issues, so the entire family and neighborhood can play. Experience gratifies, but a beginner will gain skill quickly. The best surface, as here in the Rancho Santa Fe gardens of Jim and Mary Beth Crowley, is pressed sand. American parks often have a baseball diamond with dugout space or well-prepared short grass that will serve. The size of the court can be as large as space allows. The generally accepted minimum is 12 feet wide x 39 feet long (4 m x 12 m).*

RIGHT: *Enameled watering cans add color and surprise along a stone wall in front of daylilies. The brown bucket in the foreground is a well bucket.* BELOW: *Since the late 1800s, many French farmers have been making their own wine; we made our own until the 1960s. This wine press and crusher are typical of the size of equipment needed.*

the house that would become our home in California—deep in Carmel Valley, where out of every window I see mountains that remind me of the Pyrenees—I started planting trees,

even before all the crates were unpacked. You cannot speed up time. Just as people and cultures can absorb change only so fast, trees can establish roots only at the pace nature dictates. In honor of my children, Carla, Léhéna and Olivier, I planted olive trees—320 of them along the back and west side of the property.

This is the third house I've owned, and always I've started the planting before dealing with changes desired for the house itself. Everyone pitches in. It is a sign for each of us that we are putting down roots, that we are marrying ourselves to a vision we have of our future, that we are growing a life.

When I was a boy, in the Pyrénées Atlantique, we didn't have a lawn or flower garden. We had an orchard with cherry, plum, apple, pear and walnut trees; and a vegetable garden with beans, peas, tomatoes, lettuce, melons, potatoes, garlic, onions, shallots and every other vegetable we could grow. We had fields for flax (to make linen) and grains (to make flour and to feed the animals). In the spring and summer, we grew geraniums in

Threshing boards (wood with sharp stones inserted), drawn by donkeys over cut grain, separated the kernels of grain from the chaff.

jardinières in front of the windows, but we didn't have a flower garden or a wide expanse of lawn. There wasn't time to tend these; they were not *nécessaires*.

At the palaces, the royals had staff and time for beauty alone.

Most people were working on survival, though, and flowers feed only the soul, not the body as fruits and vegetables and grains do.

THE IDEA OF GARDENS OF DELIGHT—BEAUTY FOR THE SAKE OF THE SOUL—HAS BEEN POSSIBLE ONLY RELATIVELY RECENTLY.

The idea of gardens of delight—beauty for the sake of the soul—has been possible only relatively recently. Before there could be the luxury of time all the way down to the middle class, the results of the Industrial Revolution first had to be absorbed by a very large percentage of the world population. Even in Europe today, most gardens are in public spaces—plazas, parks, arboretums, conservatories, et cetera—because cities in Europe formed hundreds, even thousands, of years before the consequences of the Industrial Revolution had percolated to the point that the concept of "ornamental plants" was widespread. Except on celebratory boulevards in major cities, the towns and villages of Europe do not have "street trees" marching along their lengths nor flower beds highlighting the corners. France is famous for her window boxes overflowing with geraniums and her abundance of "kitchen gardens," but these are purposeful—for protection from mosquitoes and for cooking.

America developed later than Europe, forming most of its city and village infrastructures after the concept of private gardens followed the time-releasing energy of the Industrial Revolution and while open space was abundant. American homes have front lawns larger than most European home sites, plus back gardens, side gardens, sunrooms, houseplants and private greenhouses! Not everyone does, of course, but taking the large look, comparing Europe with America generally, Americans have private gardens way beyond the number and size Europeans have, even in the

Designed to carry hay to animals in the field during the winter, this wheelbarrow is made of châtaignier *(chestnut), with the wheel wrapped in iron for strength.*

RIGHT: During the heyday of fonte d'art (1840–80), the best foundries competed with a rush of new products by adapting everything they could to cast iron. Bancs de jardin (garden benches) fit the bill, this one encircling an ancient tree in the California garden of Frank and Marilyn Dorsa. OPPOSITE: This table invites you to le petit déjeuner (breakfast) as the morning sun warms. Café au lait (coffee with hot milk) is on the way. The linens are "Jan de Luz Noir." The chêne (oak) table with iron legs is from a bistro in Bordeaux.

ABOVE: Cast-iron vases, these in the upright Roman style, were mounted on pillars at entrances to impart a sense of solidity. RIGHT: This cast-iron cross, made in 1880, is today in an outdoor chapel at a private home. Made during fonte d'art *primarily for the Catholic Church, few come into the market.*

LEFT: *The cast-iron frame on this marble-top table is from an old treadle (foot pedal) sewing machine.* BELOW: *Cast-iron* jardinières *were always curvaceously footed, in the spirit of Louis XVI. The terra-cotta pot behind the* jardinière *probably held olives at one time. The* vases d'Anduze, *named after the village in France where they are made, always carry the signature ribbon incrustation.*

suburbs. It is a consequence of timing, of different possibilities being available at a particular time, not a moral judgment. I see it as another way America is lucky and forgets to remember.

Many customers come to the store looking only for outdoor architectural elements, especially in the spring and summer. They look for benches, vases, fountains, wishing wells, stone sentinels—any artifact that will add interest to the garden.

BELOW: I can't imagine how drab France would be if the fonte d'art movement (see "Discovering Passion" chapter) had not brought iron into acceptance as capable of elegance. The lovely gate and the matching balconies at the home of Jim and Mary BethCrowley are in a typically French blue. RIGHT: The cast- iron balconies are better seen here. The entry walk is in Burgundy stone.

RIGHT: This iron and wood gate was, in 1870, the front door to a hôtel particulier. It now provides access between two sections of a southern California garden.
OPPOSITE: These 12-foot (3,65 m) pillars with colonnes ioniques in Régence style are about 180 years old and give a strong presence for a grand entrance.

Customers who are remodeling or beginning new construction generally also include the garden in their plans. I like that in America the garden is as much a part of creating a home, the spirit of sanctuary, as is a hearth.

Fountains and wishing wells are the most desired garden accoutrements. Now, as in the past, the best place for a well or fountain is right out front. In fact, it's important to understand that all fountains were first, by purpose, wells—sources of water—not in today's parlance "waterscapes."

ABOVE: *Six or seven months after installation in Dana Beach's Salinas, California, garden, the new fountain is taking on the shadowing and texture of age.*
RIGHT: *This well, from a* maison de maître *(country house), had only its* monolithe margelle *(round top from a single stone) and* poulie en fer forgé *(iron pulley) still* sound and working. For installation at La Rusticana Vineyards for Frank and Marilyn Dorsa, we chose limestone slabs from Provence to match the color, then faceted the stones to build the slightly octagonal base needed to fit the margelle.

If the front of the house doesn't provide appropriate space, though, other placements can be beautiful, too. Just give fountains and wells a little distance, if you can. Do not crowd them. They are intended to support activity.

Also, do not be afraid to adapt. Richard Wax had a ram's head he liked from a half-destroyed *haut-relief* (deeply carved ornament, in this case originally a *chapiteau de pilier*). What to do? He placed a tiny 150-year-old limestone *chapelle* on top, creating a protected spot for candlelight next to his outdoor Jacuzzi. It's a lovely adaptation, and singular (see page 136). There are many approaches to beauty, and the ones you discover or construct for yourself are the ones that will please you the most.

Another customer has a life-size replica of Tintin (see page 137) enjoying permanent guest status, waiting for sunset at his seaside home. A sense of humor is never out of place, especially in a garden intended to surprise and delight.

> THERE ARE MANY APPROACHES TO BEAUTY, AND THE ONES YOU DISCOVER OR CONSTRUCT FOR YOURSELF ARE THE ONES THAT WILL PLEASE YOU THE MOST.

This fall, we will take the first harvest from the olive trees we planted. The first few years after planting, we stripped the fruit from the trees as it appeared, encouraging the trees to put all their energy into forming deep roots and strong limb structure. Now that the trees are established and robust, we are letting the fruit grow and ripen. It looks like we will have a good crop, and are going to press the oil in a small home olive press I found. We will bottle our own olive oil, create a new family tradition and be able to share the bounty of earth and nature with friends. What could be better?

Surrounded by lavenders and boxwood, this fountain, the one discussed in the Foreword, is a typical octagonal village fountain. In their original placements, the low profile of octagonal fountains allowed animals to drink and villagers to draw water. The iron crossbars support the buckets while they sit filling under the spout. The column is called a moine *(monk) because it stands erect, observing everything without saying a word.*

ABOVE: *To my eye, the inclusion of the adapted* haut-relief *and truly old rocks make this Jacuzzi more relaxing than if it were only modern. The privacy of a tall wall helps too.*
LEFT: *This wall fountain, from the 1700s, is Régence (signified by the shell motif). The* monolithe *trough is large enough for horses to drink comfortably. The wall is new, designed and crafted for Frank and Marilyn Dorsa to feel a century or two old.*

Superhero and Belgian world reporter Tintin (notice his houpette—haircut featuring a sporty upright tuft) sits with his dog, Milou (Snowy), looking out to sea, perhaps recalling his fantastic adventures. An icon throughout Europe and the world, Tintin began traveling with Milou in 1929, finding exotic adventures in Russia, the Congo, South America, the Himalayas, even the moon—wherever his Belgian creator, Hergé, sent the itinerant hero. Written and expressively illustrated for children but followed by adults as well, the twenty-four tales always end happily. Hergé was, in life, George Remi, a newspaper editor who loved drawing and one day took a lark in developing the first Tintin adventure—another instance of how following one's passion responsibly can lead to wonderful consequences.

THE FRENCH
TOUCH

A PASSION FOR THE ECLECTIC—A MIXING AND MATCHING WITH EQUAL PARTS PUR-POSE AND ADMIRATION—ALLOWS A PERSON TO SEEK QUALITY AND DURABILITY WHILE ENJOYING A SENSE OF PERSONAL TASTE. IN FACT, CRAFTSMANSHIP AND ARTISTRY REQUIRE SELF-ASSURANCE. ACCORDINGLY, *THE FRENCH TOUCH* INVITES BOLD SELF-EXPRESSION IN THE SELECTION AND PLACEMENT OF EVERY PARTICULAR PIECE. ONLY THROUGH THESE PERSONAL CHOICES DOES THE REINCARNATION OF THE ANTIQUE OR ARCHITECTURAL ELEMENT TRULY COME ALIVE AGAIN. SAVING THE OLD AND BEAUTIFUL TO SERVE ANEW IS BUSINESS FOR ME, YES; BUT MORE THAN THAT, IT IS A PERSONAL ETHIC, AND DEEPLY GRATIFYING. The climate and geography of the Central Coast of California is sufficiently evocative of Pyrénées Atlantique

*Truly inviting is this deep,
sloping copper tub lined
with étain (pewter) for
smoothness, mounted
above ever-warm coil heat.
Individuality is central
to personality.*

that I can feel "at home" one minute and "homesick" the next. I am well planted in life here now, with my family, business and dreams all thriving. I travel back to France often enough to be reminded of the wonders of my Basque homeland and the reasons I love California and America. A fortunate man is well tied to his past and his future. I do not understand why some people try so hard to run from their shadows. First, it is impossible. That is reason enough. Second, if it were possible, you would be losing part of yourself. Understanding, acceptance and memory are stronger than denial and numbness. I really do believe it is good to follow Emerson's advice and try to live ahead of your mistakes: ". . . *Some blunders and absurdities, no doubt (creep) in; forget them as soon as you can. Tomorrow is a new day; begin it well and serenely with too high a spirit to be encumbered with your old nonsense.*"

When we were still new to the area and looking for a house, I would drive around, getting to know the neighborhoods. There are plenty of wonderful neighborhoods in the Central Coast, some too rich for my wallet, but it is interesting to study the houses—how they are constructed and what people do with them. This kind of activity is called a "busman's holiday," I think, as you say in America.

I love this house! It would have been easier to forego the curved entrées *(supporting beams at the front of an entrance structure), but it wouldn't have been so purely Norman, so truly itself. For a creation to stand singularly as itself, it must feel integrated in every respect. This house exemplifies quality from every angle and in every step of construction. I respect what it requires to maintain quality. Humans can sometimes hit upon an exceptional result; it is the way of inspiration and what some call happenstance. For anything man-made to stay exceptional, though, requires, first, intention and, then, the follow-through of attention to details. The process of duplication and repetition will degrade any effort unless fresh focus is given constantly.*

One house I saw simply fascinated me. It is stunning, so French in its design and execution—from the slate roof, *lucarnes* (eyebrow dormer windows), zinc spires, deep eaves, shuttered windows and *colombages* (wood cross-structures) like Basque houses, to the movement of the rooflines that remind me of the building we created for the Basque *éco-musée*. And the superb quality of the post-and-beam construction! It is a well-conceived, well-made and exceptionally inviting, homey residence. The more you study it, the more impressive its quality.

Then one day I discovered, again, that I live under lucky stars. My wife, Brigitte, asked me if I would deliver a clock to its new home. *Bien sûr.* I headed out, map in hand, to an address that meant nothing to me on paper, toward the scent of the sea, until I found

myself in the driveway of the very house that fascinates me. Smack my brow, what were the odds?

There was a Willys Jeep standing at attention out front. I smiled, knowing I'd have stories to share with its owner because I'm a nut about cars, too. Then I met a sweet, cordial, extremely intelligent and cultured man who not only owned the house but had built it.

While I installed the *boulangerie mobile* clock in the kitchen,

Above: This is one seriously built house. Near to the sea, the stone, the sturdy shutters and strong iron strap hinges are shelter against storms. OPPOSITE: These amazing roof entanglements are typically Norman-style architetture. Complex is not always complicated. It can be simply lovely.

this gracious, welcoming gentleman engaged me. We talked La Cornue stoves (the "Ferrari" of stoves, if one doesn't mind mixing countries in one's metaphor), Burgundy limestone, Louis XIII fireplaces, Normandy architecture, the meaning of sanctuary and the value of quality. Surrounded by the robust strength of a house suited to the man who built it, I met someone whose self-assurance permitted openness and kindliness. Amid the harmony of the colors and textures natural to the man and this home, I realized again how just going about your business can bring surprises that add interest and levity to life through new friendships and sharing.

So, you see, my theory: Life is an adventure, a canvas on which to express ourselves—as this house does for this man, and as every home does for any property owner who also becomes a *home*owner with a sense of individual identity. Recognizing style as personal expression allows one to be idiosyncratic. Genuine style must arise from within, from decisions you make according to your own lights.

When you bring objects from the past into a house, you add a personal touch. It's not

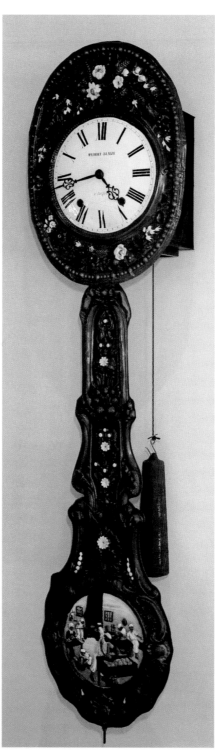

LEFT: The Swiss had their cuckoo clocks for whimsy; the French have their elegant animated pendulum clocks with scenes appropriate to every room. This one is a boulangerie mobile (animated clock demonstrating a bakery). The pendulum keeps the time and activates a counterweight inside the pendulum, which keeps the baker kneading bread, all the day long. Other animations feature a mother rocking her baby, a smithy working his forge, men drinking wine. The decorative flowers are painted laiton repoussé (pressed brass); the face is enamel. Most popular during the mid-19th century, all French animated clocks were made in the villages of Morbier and Morez in the French Jura Mountains bordering Switzerland. A few rare ones are full-month clocks; most are eight-day clocks, ringing a bell or a gong on the hour and half-hour. They repeat the hour after three minutes, which is why they are also called "prayer clocks."

FAR LEFT: Arched doorways are another telltale sign of quality construction in this home. Through the French doors to the patio, you can just make out a marble-topped table de boucherie (display table for meats from a delicatessen). The textures, colors and prints here are all typically French.

LEFT: *In the Basque country, water from wells was stored in* cruches *(water jugs) in special racks. The small space at the end is for the drinking cup. Under the bench are* pots de confit *(food storage pots). Colorful* parefeuille *terra-cotta paving is so handsome that, although its main asset is its strength, it is sometimes used as indoor ceiling tile because it carries an expanse so beautifully. The* dalle *(rain gutter) includes a* trop plein *(reservoir) to accommodate torrential rains.*
OPPOSITE: Alcôves *for beds were adopted in the days of palaces, when a bed sitting in a giant room wasn't particularly cozy. An* alcôve *feels more protected, warmer, and provides a place for* vêtements de nuit *(night clothes) and extra bedding. The style of the curves and color and design here are Louis XVI.*

really a style. You can place an art deco coffee table in front of a Renaissance fireplace and not yield to either period. History defines some periods of tastes—Renaissance, Régence, Empire, Art Nouveau, et cetera—but history does not define the person, or at least it shouldn't. Style isn't following someone else's rules; it is shaping, grooming one's own point of view. A house becomes a home by becoming a singular expression of one's own spirit and needs.

These personal touches can be simple or extraordinary. I work with people who can afford a lot of self-expression, but as with the point I made earlier (see page 84) about overstuffed rooms where more for more's sake is mistaken for merit, quality is what counts, not volume.

ABOVE: This walnut panetière *is a* claire-voie
*(one can see through the spindles) and is intended to
be mounted on a wall.* RIGHT: *France has many
culinary accessories. The* panetière *is one—a device
for storing bread in the* salle á manger *(dining
room). The bronze* chandeliers *(candlesticks) are
Restauration period. The* lustre *(chandelier) is
new; also in the style of the Restauration.*

For instance, while I mentioned earlier that wells and fountains were originally sources of water, tools for survival, Bruce and Karyn DeBoer nonetheless adapted a small but strong well in their Saratoga, California, yard as a large, intriguing *jardinière*. Adaptation is the stuff of life, growth's most necessary ingredient. Express yourself!

The only caution is that the French touch requires thought and an eye for detail. The details produce the result. Intention is all well and good, as we say in America, but without

BELOW: Cranking a log would require strong arms. You can see here the channeling where years of work have been done. Now transplanted to a suburban yard, this well serves as a gigantic jardinière. *Adaptation is a mark of creativity.* OPPOSITE: *Parquet floors deserve space—the better to admire the design. The concept of laying floors in intricately cut designs pre-dates* le château de Versailles, *for even before 1600, architects and workers realized they could make more money by doing more work. Architects would design the most labor-intensive designs for their best customers. When a madness for everything Versailles swept the country, patterns for* parquet de Versailles *became standardized at approximately 3.3 feet x 3.3 feet x 1.5 inches (98 cm x 98 cm x 3,8 cm).* INSET: *The grain of the wood in this Versailles panel develops an almost three-dimensional sense of basket weave.*

attention to detail in the follow-through, no intention survives process any more than an idea can be said to be as important as a deed.

I didn't coin the term *the French touch*. I'm sure it predates me by a long while. It seems like an American coinage. Simple words, yet difficult to translate, unless you have an understanding of French sensibility, which begins with an appreciation of quality, supported by the small touches, the details, that define a setting in a singular way.

I admit it: I like beautiful things. I grew up among them, surrounded by people who taught me the skill of editing one's environment, of eliminating the things that no longer inspire or develop one's inner strength or reflect positively the spirit and vision one continuously develops for oneself. This is what I mean about style being the grooming of point of view. If one knows and understands oneself, accepts and appreciates oneself, self-expression is natural and necessary.

Every time I buy something for the business or for myself, I only buy what's real; only good stuff. It's automatic. Money is an issue, of course, as it always is, for money is a resource to be respected. In given circumstances, I prefer a small diamond but a real and beautiful one, rather than anything poorly executed or fake. I buy only beautiful pieces. A trained eye has an abhorrence for sham.

I teach this principle about quality—always quality, only quality—to my children, too. It is a matter of

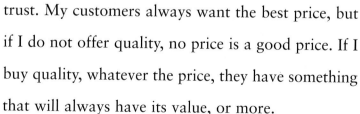

ABOVE: *This brass-trimmed mahogany vitrine, built with the ease of a steamer trunk in mind, holds options at eye level. What we want to know: What is in the orange boxes?* LEFT: *Ties by the gross, almost. One pleasure of custom building is the chance to enjoy your passions.* OPPOSITE: *The deep, enveloping warmth of a full-size cast-iron porcelain claw-foot tub by a sunny window is Mary Beth Crowley's dream of luxury.*

trust. My customers always want the best price, but if I do not offer quality, no price is a good price. If I buy quality, whatever the price, they have something that will always have its value, or more.

So, *bon courage*. Take a chance with yourself and with your instincts. Use the old to soften the new or to add strength to it. The tender and the robust can complement each other, whether linens or limestone.

This counter from the early 1900s was originally a display counter in a charcuterie (deli-catessen) in Paris. The structure is made of wood, then faced, paneled and topped with marble. The center design on the front is an inlay of terra-cotta. It now serves as a room divider, sheltering a view of the stairs that descend to the wine cellar. Notice the hotte en osier (rattan harvest basket) on the wall behind.

The French touch calls for a mixture, juxtapositions and layers of complementary items—sumptuous fabrics amid strongly constructed tapestries, weathered woods next to gleaming glass, iron wrought with muscle and imagination standing on the humblest old stone, earthenware made more useful with a delicately crafted pewter handle—all toward showing how the necessary is fulfilled by the unexpected.

"Life is a tough slog . . . all the knocks and hard things. You have to get out there and hustle and hassle. Listen and watch. Learn. . . ." I heard that statement on American television. I don't see much television, and wasn't actually watching that day; only heard part of a television interview while in an airport lounge on the way back to France. The voice was Irish and old, even elderly. It sounded worn but not burdened; wise. I guess my mind switched attention because the statement reminded me of something I had said to my children before I left for that trip. It was something to the effect that I am overjoyed with them, with life, and that I wish for everybody to have the same quality of life, the same spirit of living as I have, because I have a great life, mostly because I appreciate its surprises so much. I told them, to explain why I had to leave again, that everyone has to work, and work hard for personal satisfaction. "Hustle and hassle . . . listen and watch . . . learn," as this wise man was saying, because it is in the hustle and the hassle, the listening and the learning that we find how to create opportunities to express ourselves in singular ways.

This is living, and I wish a full life for you; one full of beauty, passion for the things you assign to yourself as important, and ever an adventure of discovery, of the substance of history and the power of imagination.

Leiho *is the Basque word for* "window." *The white field is woven in* damas *(damask), requiring a tone-on-tone weaving with dimension (relief). The stripes, here in French blue, are woven in* serge, *to give the stripes a flatter feel. All Jan de Luz linens are heirloom quality, with colors that are woven, never printed. This table sits in front of a Louis XV–period limestone mantel with* trumeau. *The clock is Napoléon III, and the cast-iron* coupe *is a Val d'Osne from the 1860s.*

RESOURCES

JAN DE LUZ RETAIL STORES

Jan de Luz-Carmel
Dolores between Ocean and
Seventh
P.O. Box 1115
Carmel, CA 93921
831.622.7621
jandeluz@aol.com
www.jandeluz.com

Jan de Luz-Carmel Valley
4 East Carmel Valley Road
Carmel Valley, CA 93924
831.659.7966
sales@jandeluz.com
www.jandeluz.com

Jan de Luz-St. Helena
1219 Main Street
St. Helena, CA 94574
707.963.1550
jdlsh@jandeluz.com
www.jandeluz.com

Jan de Luz-New York
345 West Broadway
New York, NY 10013
212.343.9911
jandeluz_ny@hotmail.com

Jan de Luz-Scottsdale
8787 N. Scottsdale Road
Scottsdale, AZ 75253
480.778.0255
info@azjandeluz.com

ARCHITECTS AND DESIGNERS

Michael Bolton
Bolton Design Group, Inc.
P.O. Box 5488
Carmel, CA 93921
831.622.2550
mbolton@boltondesigngroup.com

Paul E. Davis, AIA
The Paul Davis Partnership
286 El Dorado
Monterey, CA 93940
831.373.2784
pauldavis@sbcglobal.net

David P. Howerton
Hart Howerton
One Union Street – 3rd Floor
San Francisco, CA 94111
415.439.2200
dhowerton@harthowerton.com

International Design Group
John E. Matthams
Jun A. Sillano, AIA
721 Lighthouse Avenue
Pacific Grove, CA 93950
831.646.1261
jemidg@jemidg.com

Michael Layne
Michael Layne & Associates
1432 Main Street
St. Helena, CA 95474
707.967.9474
mikewine@aol.com

Wayne Leong, AIA
P.O. Box 2
St. Helena, CA 94574
707.963.5461
info@leongarch.com
www.leongarch.com

William Hefner, AIA
William Hefner Architecture
  and Interiors
5820 Wilshire Blvd, Ste 500
Los Angeles, CA 90036
323.931.1365
mbox@williamhefner.com

Bing Hu
H&S International
17785 N. Pacesetter Way, #800
Scottsdale, AZ 85255
480.585.6898
BHu@handsinternational.com

Darrell James, AIA
P.O. Box 2557
Carmel, CA 93921
831.277.6541
www.darrelljames.net

Donald McBride
P.O. Box 1932
Carmel, CA 93921
831.626.4266
csmithinsserv@aol.com

John Sorrell
Sorrell Design
1115 Coast Village Road
Montecito, CA 93108
805.565.2288

CONTRACTORS AND SUBS

Greg Blackwell
Greg Blackwell Homes
505 Gordon Avenue
San Jose, CA 95127
408.667.9123

Scott Coulter
Old World Finishes
P.O. Box 2002
Seaside, CA 93955
831.393.9525
Kcou102823@aol.com

Richie DeAmaral
Richard DeAmaral Masonry, Inc.
2890 Rancho Rea Road
Aromas, CA 95004
831.726.7032
DeAmaralmasonry@cs.com

Bruce DeBoer
DeBoer Construction
14310 Lutheria Way
Saratoga, CA 95070
408.867.2071
deboer1@earthlink.net

Ray Marzorini
Marzorini-Maschmeyer Masonry
9755 Hillview Terrace
Salinas, CA 93907
831.663.3115

Tim Scherer
Regency Construction Co., Inc.
21 W. Carmel Valley Road
Carmel Valley, CA 93924
831.659.5881
regency@redshift.com

Alfie Wardle
California Construction Mgmt
137 East Carmel Valley Road
Carmel Valley, CA 93924
831.659.4286
alfiewardle00@prodigy.net

Don Whitaker
The Golden Hammer
2072 Sunset Drive
Pacific Grove, CA 93950
831.372.8585
don.whitaker2@gte.net

INTERIOR DESIGNERS

Linda Applewhite
Linda Applewhite & Associates
828 Mission Avenue
San Rafael, CA 94901
415.456.2757
www.lindaapplewhite.com

Kim Brockinton
D'Yquem
5919 Kavanaugh
Little Rock, AR 72207
501.661.7600
lisagass@sbcglobal.net

Karyn DeBoer
Tollgate Interiors
14310 Lutheria Way
Saratoga, CA 95070
408.741.5177

Orlando Diaz-Azcuy
Orlando Diaz-Azcuy Design
Associates
210 Post Street, 9th Floor
San Francisco, CA 94108
415.362.4500
oda@odada.net

Charles Gruwell
Charles Gruwell Design
4620 South Arville Street, Ste H
Las Vegas, CA 89103
702.270.6666
cg@charlesgruwelldesign.com

Linda L. Floyd, Inc.
Design & Decoration
1791 Montemar Way
San Jose, CA 95125
408.978.6542
lfloyd7258@aol.com

Barbara Grivin Hoskinson
Rose Bank Design
2995 Woodside Road, Ste 400
Woodside, CA 94062
650.366.3332
hillbarb@sbcglobal.net

Tracey McKee Interior Design
5219 North Casa Blanca Drive
Paradise Valley, AZ 85253
480.945.3599
tmckeeinteriors@aol.com

Marie Christine Peterson
Chelsea Court Designs
100 Los Gatos-Saratoga Road,
  Ste D
Los Gatos, CA 95032
408.399.7720
info@chelseacourtdesigns.com

Michelle Pheasant
Michelle Pheasant Design, Inc.
225 Cannery Row, Ste I
Monterey, CA 93940
831.372.2092
michellempdinc@aol.com

Wendy Posard
Wendy Posard & Associates
305 San Anselmo Avenue
San Anselmo, CA 94960
415.456.2020

Schneider Fox & Associates
John J. Schneider
Luba Fox
P.O. Box 1457
Pebble Beach, CA 93953
831.620.1738
schneiderdesign@earthlink.net

John Charles H Stewart
John Stewart Designs
550 Fifteenth Street
San Francisco, CA 94103
415.550.7300
info@johnstewartdesigns.com

Richard Winsberg
101 S. Robinson Blvd, Ste 206
Los Angeles, CA 90048
310.278.9111
rwinsberg@earthlink.net

LANDSCAPE DESIGNERS

Greg Grisamore
Greg Grisamore Design
1137 Bayside Drive
Corona del Mar, CA 92625
949.644.4719
design@ggrisamore.com

Anne H. Howerton
Hart Howerton
One Union Street – 3rd Floor
San Francisco, CA 94111
415.439.2200
ahowerton@harthowerton.com

Michael B. Yandle
5 Ross Common
P.O. Box 1695
Ross, CA 94957
415.699.6931
mbyandle@earthlink.net

PHOTOGRAPHY

Tom O'Neal
Tom O'Neal Photography
P.O. Box 1520
Carmel Valley, CA 93924
831.659.5040
tom@tgophoto.com
www.tgophoto.com

RESTORATIONS

Walter Loeliger
50 Flight Road
Carmel Valley, CA 93924
831.659.8646

Jan de Luz